THE INSTITUTE OF ECONOMICS
OF
THE BROOKINGS INSTITUTION

PUBLICATION No. 86

THE BROOKINGS INSTITUTION

The Brookings Institution—Devoted to Public Service through Research and Training in the Social Sciences—was incorporated on December 8, 1927. Broadly stated, the Institution has two primary purposes: the first is to aid constructively in the development of sound national policies; and the second is to offer training of a super-graduate character to students of the social sciences. The Institution will maintain a series of co-operating institutes, equipped to carry out comprehensive and inter-related research projects.

The responsibility for the final determination of the Institution's policies and its program of work and for the administration of its endowment is vested in a self-perpetuating board of trustees. It is the function of the trustees to make possible the conduct of scientific research under the most favorable conditions, and to safeguard the independence of the research staff in the pursuit of their studies and in the publication of the results of such studies. It is not a part of their function to determine, control, or influence the conduct of particular investigations or the conclusions reached; but only to approve the principal fields of investigation to which the available funds are to be allocated, and to satisfy themselves with reference to the intellectual competence and scientific integrity of the staff. Major responsibility for "formulating general policies and co-ordinating the activities of the various divisions of the Institution" is vested in the president. The by-laws provide also that "there shall be an advisory council selected by the president from among the scientific staff of the Institution and representing the different divisions of the Institution."

BOARD OF TRUSTEES

NAZI EUROPE
AND
WORLD TRADE

BY
CLEONA LEWIS

ASSISTED BY
JOHN C. McCLELLAND

THE BROOKINGS INSTITUTION
WASHINGTON, D.C.
1941

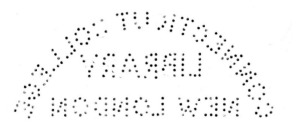

Printed in the United States of America
George Banta Publishing Company
Menasha, Wisconsin

DIRECTOR'S PREFACE

So loud has been the talk of *lebensraum* and so swift and spectacular the success of Germany's territorial conquests that it is easy to assume that redrawing the map of Europe achieves economic self-sufficiency for the Third Reich. In this volume, Miss Lewis and her associates have subjected this assumption to quantitative checking. The conclusions are severely factual in form. But the process of definition, selection, cumulation, and comparison involved in this statistical undertaking and the technical comment by which the figures are accompanied afford a perspective and sidelight which facilitate sound interpretation.

Writing in times like these, an author runs the risk of defining his inquiry or selecting its area of coverage in terms which may suddenly have their significance changed or impaired by the swift march of new developments. It may be that tomorrow we shall all feel the need of adding up the figures for some area having other geographical boundaries. But by its very nature, continental Europe will remain a region of distinctive economic significance in terms of its limitations and potentialities. Furthermore, the conclusions to which the study of the "Nazi area" points will shed considerable light on the stability or instability, the aloofness or degree of collaboration which must in future characterize this area, whatever the outcome of military struggle or political organization.

EDWIN G. NOURSE
Director

Institute of Economics
May 1941   97806

v

AUTHOR'S ACKNOWLEDGMENTS

The author wishes to acknowledge her indebtedness to the following associates—Werner Baer, Al Costanzo, Alfred E. Kahn, Carl Kreider, John C. McClelland, Ruth Russell, and Erich Schiff—who spent some time on the collection and analysis of materials for a survey of the trade and resources of the principal trade areas of the world. While that project was laid aside when the invasion of the Netherlands was followed by the defeat of the French forces, group discussions of many questions of definition and method, of data sources and choice of material, contributed greatly to the speedy preparation of the present volume. Miss Russell also helped with the compilation of data for the Nazi area, particularly in connection with Chapters II and III, and Mr. McClelland has assisted with the compilation and analysis of data for the whole study.

We are greatly indebted to Mrs. M. B. Price, of the Bureau of Mines, for valuable aid in the collection of data for Chapter IV and to J. C. McGrath and J. W. Furness for assistance in the analysis of that chapter. We are also under obligation to Henry J. Tasca for suggestions with regard to Chapter V, to J. C. Nellis for assistance in connection with the section on timber and woodpulp, and to the art editors of *Life* for the base map used in showing the direction of Nazi Europe's trade. Finally, we wish to thank the many other experts, particularly in the Department of Agriculture, who advised with us on a variety of technical questions.

CLEONA LEWIS

CONTENTS

CONTENTS

INTRODUCTION

Nazi Europe, or the area now more or less effectually controlled by Nazi Germany, includes most of continental Europe. Only the states under Soviet domination have so far escaped being drawn within the German orbit. Along with the two European Axis powers, it takes in the territories added to Germany prior to the war, those invaded since war began, and those that nominally still maintain their independence. Its population, according to 1937 figures, is roughly two and a half times that of the United States. Its area is only a little more than half as large.

The future for this conglomerate of states undoubtedly will depend on the circumstances in which hostilities come to an end. The Germans have made clear their intention of forging these states, or even more, into a political and economic union—but one that differs materially from the much-discussed ideal of a "United States of Europe." That utopian dream visualizes a voluntary association and co-operation of autonomous nations. Nazi Europe, on the contrary, looks toward a future dominated entirely by a "master (German) race." Exploited for the benefit of this favored population there will be the subject states. The latter will carry on their more important activities—including their trade and industry—in accordance with blueprints provided from Berlin, where the economic and political policies for all will be formulated.

Of particular interest at this time is the threat frequently voiced that, if not by military means then through her economic control over all of continental Europe west of Russia, Germany will be in a position to dominate the trade of the world, including that of the United States. This implies that because of the volume and value of her trade, Nazi Europe would, in most cases, play the great game of world trade with dice loaded in her favor. In essence, this would mean either that the area is able to supply its own basic consumptive requirements, and therefore can buy abroad or refrain from buying as it chooses; or that it is in an extraordinarily advantageous position as regards the export commodities—or services—it offers in world markets, and as regards its principal sources of supply. It is this underlying assumption that we propose to examine in the pages which follow.

Put briefly, the question to be considered is whether—judged by past performances—the resources of this area are of such a character that independence of foreign sources of supply is likely to be realized; or if self-sufficiency is lacking, whether the area enjoys extraordinary advantages in the field of trade. We say "judged by past performances," since it is impossible to know now what the future output of the fields, forests, mines, and factories of the combined area might be under a new régime—whether the area is again broken into separate states, or unified under German control, or joined in some kind of voluntary federation. But, whatever the outcome of the war may be, time will be required to repair war damages to physical plant and equipment, and to recover from the other economic and social effects of the war.

Specifically, the questions considered in this analysis are:

1. Is the area independent with respect to foodstuffs?

2. Is the area self-sufficient as to agricultural raw materials and forestry products?

3. Does the area produce all the industrial minerals normally required?

4. What are the primary foreign sources of supply from which import requirements are met?

5. What exportable surpluses are available, and what are the principal outlets for European exports?

6. What other sources of income are available for meeting income requirements?

In short, the analysis is focused on the international trade position of a Nazi-dominated Europe. Conceiving this area as a single country, and regarding the trade between its component parts as internal trade, we seek to determine what problems it faces with regard to external trade. However, we do not attempt to discuss the problems which would be involved in unifying and co-ordinating the economic life of continental Europe under a centralized, planned economy.

The two years that we have selected for gauging the productive resources and trade of the area are 1929 and 1937. The former was one of the few prosperous years made possible by the stabilizing effects of the Dawes plan and of large American loans. The year 1937 was one of great business activity in Germany, and one of reasonably normal trade relations. That is to say, the economies of Germany and neighboring states had not as yet been greatly distorted by the purchase and storage of goods for war purposes. The analysis thus will leave out of consideration all of the difficult problems of reorganization and reconstruction—physical, economic, commercial, and political. And it will take no account of whatever increased volume of production may materialize in the future.

We do not know how the war will end, or what the future political and economic organization of Europe will be. But since the great concern of the moment is over the potentiality of a German-dominated continent of Europe, we shall assume, for the purposes of this analysis, that Germany will, at the end of the war, control all of continental Europe west of Russia and the states in the Russian sphere.

The countries included in such a Nazi Europe would be as follows, in alphabetical order: Albania, Austria, Belgium-Luxemburg, Bulgaria, Czechoslovakia, Denmark, France, Germany, Greece, Hungary, Italy, the Netherlands, Norway, Poland (in some chapters, only half of the trade of this country being included with the German area, and the rest with the Russian), Portugal, Rumania, Spain, Sweden, Switzerland, and Yugoslavia —20 in all. Turkey, whose independence has been maintained, is omitted from the list because by far the greater part of her territory and resources are in Mediterranean Asia.

In order to show the extent to which the trade requirements of the area would be modified if Germany should gain control of Turkey and other countries bordering the Mediterranean on the south, we also present brief summaries of the trade of these countries—including Algeria, Morocco, Tunisia, Libya, and the Tangier Zone, and also Egypt, Turkey, Syria, Lebanon, Palestine, and Cyprus. It is a well-known fact that expansion into some of these countries would open gateways to important regions south and east—for example, to the oil of Iraq, Iran, and Russia, whose significance is indicated in the analysis of the trade in petroleum in Chapter IV.

The first chapter will show the value of the area's foreign trade by large commodity groups—food, raw materials, and manufactured goods. This furnishes a general indication of the character of domestic resources, what shortages there are, and what exportable surpluses have been produced in the two years studied. Consideration is given first to the trade of the old Reich, an area whose shortage of food and raw materials has been given by the Germans as a partial explanation for the seizure of additional territory on the continent. This is followed by a somewhat similar analysis of the larger area under discussion.

In Chapters II–IV, the food and raw-material requirements and supplies of the area are considered in terms of individual commodities. Here volume figures rather than values are given. With the element of price eliminated, the production and trade data for single commodities or narrow groups of similar commodities are combined to show the consumptive requirements of the area in comparison with the domestic supply. These chapters also show what outside sources supply Europe with her principal food and raw-material imports, and indicate how important the European market is as an outlet for exports from the principal producers of such commodities. Similarly, the destination of exports is shown for the foods and raw materials that are on an export basis.

Chapter V indicates the problems involved in financing the area's import requirements. In this connection, account is taken of the well-known fact that trade in commodities is only one of the many kinds of transactions normally carried on between the political divisions of the world. It also points briefly to the various devices by which Nazi Germany was able to secure, not only a supply of imports for current consumption, but also those stored against the prospective lean days of the present war and those used in the construction of war machines and equipment.

Chapter VI shows the sources and destinations of the area's aggregate imports and exports—in value terms. It also shows the relative importance of this trade to each of the large geographic regions of the world, and to individual countries.

A concluding chapter briefly summarizes our findings and relates them to the postwar problems of the Western Hemisphere.

CHAPTER I

PRODUCTION SHORTAGES INDICATED BY COMMODITY TRADE

Speaking before the Reichstag on January 30, 1939, Herr Hitler proposed two ways by which Germany might meet her chronic shortage of domestically produced raw materials and foodstuffs: first, expand exports, with a view to increasing the volume of her imports; second, extend her "living space," thereby achieving independence of foreign foodstuffs.[1] Since then, his armies have been used to widen Germany's so-called living space. The questions to be considered in this chapter are: (1) the extent to which Germany is dependent on outside sources for food and raw materials; and (2) whether, by enlarging the area under her control, Germany has attained independence of foreign raw materials and foodstuffs.

I. FOREIGN TRADE OF THE OLD REICH

The production shortages to which Hitler referred are clearly indicated by the foreign trade of the old Reich. Food and raw materials constitute the greater part of the imports taken into Germany, while manufactures account for the larger part of its exports. So far as these characteristics are concerned, the trade has shown considerable stability over a long period of years—whether

---

[1] *New York Times*, Jan. 31, 1939. At that time the Reich had already annexed Austria (March 1938), and both the Sudetenland and Memel (October 1938). The following October (1939) saw the annexation of Western Poland.

it has been at the high levels reached in 1913 and the 1920's, or at the lows of 1932 and subsequent years.

Food and raw materials usually have accounted for around 90 per cent of total imports. Manufactured goods made up the small remainder. The relative importance of these three large classes of commodities in the import trade of the old Reich is shown below. The first three

CHARACTER OF GERMAN IMPORTS, 1913, 1925–37[a]

Year	Percentage Distribution of Total			Value (in millions)	
	Food[b]	Raw Materials[c]	Manu-factures[d]	Marks	Dollars[e]
1913........	38.2	52.1	9.7	10,770	2,565
1925........	42.3	47.9	9.8	12,362	2,942
1926........	46.5	44.5	9.0	10,001	2,380
1927........	39.8	48.4	11.8	14,228	3,381
1928........	40.9	46.2	12.9	14,001	3,341
1929........	40.0	46.9	13.1	13,447	3,202
1930........	40.7	45.7	13.6	10,393	2,479
1931........	41.4	44.2	14.4	6,727	1,590
1932........	45.7	42.4	11.9	4,667	1,108
1933........	38.8	49.2	12.0	4,204	1,283
1934........	34.7	52.4	12.9	4,451	1,753
1935........	34.5	55.7	9.8	4,159	1,674
1936........	35.5	55.1	9.4	4,218	1,700
1937........	37.4	54.4	7.3	5,468	2,198

[a] From the *Statistisches Jahrbuch fuer das Deutsche Reich*, 1938, p. 256. In 1937 a figure is given for "goods returned" amounting to 0.9 per cent of the total.
[b] Including living animals (a very small figure), and feed for animals.
[c] Both raw and processed raw materials.
[d] Finished and semi-finished goods.
[e] Converted from marks to dollars at current rates of exchange published in the *Federal Reserve Bulletin*.

columns give a percentage distribution of the total value of this trade. The last two columns show its value—in marks and dollars.

Manufactures have made up roughly 65 to 80 per cent of German exports. An analysis of the export trade is presented in the table which follows. As in the preceding import table, a percentage distribution of the trade is given by large commodity classes, followed by a statement of the total value of exports, in marks and in dollars.

CHARACTER OF GERMAN EXPORTS, 1913, 1925–37[a]

Year	Percentage Distribution of Total			Value (in millions)	
	Food[b]	Raw Materials[c]	Manu-factures[d]	Marks	Dollars[e]
1913.......	12.0	24.1	63.9	10,097	2,405
1925.......	7.2	22.9	69.9	9,290	2,211
1926.......	6.0	27.8	66.2	10,415	2,479
1927.......	5.4	25.6	69.0	10,801	2,566
1928.......	6.4	24.4	69.2	12,276	2,929
1929.......	6.5	23.5	70.0	13,483	3,210
1930.......	5.5	22.2	72.3	12,036	2,871
1931.......	5.0	20.6	74.4	9,599	2,268
1932.......	4.5	19.8	75.7	5,739	1,363
1933.......	4.6	20.3	75.1	4,871	1,487
1934.......	3.6	20.8	75.6	4,167	1,641
1935.......	2.2	20.2	77.6	4,270	1,719
1936.......	1.8	18.4	79.8	4,768	1,922
1937.......	1.5	19.0	79.5	5,911	2,376

[a] From the *Statistiscshes Jahrbuch fuer das Deutsche Reich*, 1938, p. 257.
[b] Including living animals (a very small figure), and feed for animals.
[c] Both raw and processed raw materials.
[d] Finished and semi-finished goods.
[e] Converted from marks to dollars at current rates of exchange published in the *Federal Reserve Bulletin*.

Minor shifts in the trade during recent years have not changed its essential character. Since 1933 the foreign trade of Germany has operated under increasingly stringent controls. Strenuous efforts have been made to expand the volume of imports considered indispensable for carrying through the programs of the Nazi government; and to this end, "surplus" domestic goods have been pressed upon foreign markets.

The figures given on preceding pages show that after 1932, food imports and food exports both declined in comparison with total imports and exports. Such changes probably may be explained largely by the efforts made to substitute domestic for foreign trade wherever possible, and are in line with the economies introduced following the cessation of foreign borrowing.[2] Their effects on the trade balance are, of course, off-setting in character. In fact, from 1929 forward, net imports of food represented practically a fixed percentage of the aggregate amounts receivable from all raw-material and manufactured exports.[3]

Raw materials accounted for an increasing proportion of total imports after 1932, while exports of these commodities (in comparison with total exports) showed practically no change. The contrary was true of manufactured goods: exports were increasing in relative importance; imports were falling.

These shifts have served to accentuate, not change, the existing character of German production and trade. Old Germany is still dependent on foreign sources for many raw materials and foodstuffs, and dependent on domestic manufactures for a large share of the exports that provide funds used in meeting payments on imports.

[2] During the prosperous twenties, for example, it was advantageous for one section of Germany to import foreign food, while a distant part of the country was exporting similar German goods. In the thirties, however, the obstacles offered by a long haul inside the frontiers were less important than the difficulties involved in meeting payments across the frontiers.

[3] This ratio was somewhat higher during the period when foreign borrowing provided part of the funds used in meeting payments on commodity imports.

II. TRADE OF NAZI EUROPE

Of the 20 states included in Nazi Europe, some are engaged principally in agriculture; some, like the old Reich, are highly industrialized. In relation to the German economy, therefore, some of them are complementary and some are competing in character. To arrive at tentative conclusions concerning the productive resources of the area as a whole, the trade of the several states is analyzed below by large classes of commodities.

For present purposes it is assumed that, *within* each of the commodity groups, the goods sent out by the exporting states are the kind wanted by the importing states. In short, it is assumed here that when the net exports and net imports of the 20 separate states are canceled against each other, the result will give a reasonably satisfactory picture of the trade requirements of the area as a whole. This leaves out of consideration the extent to which there are, in fact, surpluses and deficiencies of important individual commodities—a question that is discussed in Chapters II–IV.

Of the 20 component states, only 3 appear to be fully complementary to Germany in the character of their trade.

GROUP I. EXPORTERS OF FOOD AND RAW MATERIALS, IMPORTERS OF MANUFACTURES, 1937, 1929

[Net imports (+), net exports (−), in millions of dollars][a]

Country	1937				1929			
	Food	Raw Materials	Manufactures	Total	Food	Raw Materials	Manufactures	Total
Bulgaria.....	− 28.5	− 14.2	+ 37.6	− 5.1	− 8.6	− 16.0	+ 38.6	+14.0
Rumania.....	− 86.8	−108.2	+112.5	− 82.5	− 56.9	− 77.3	+138.2	+ 4.0
Yugoslavia...	− 60.4	− 40.7	+ 75.3	− 25.8	− 50.4	− 38.7	+ 83.2	− 5.9
Total......	−175.7	−163.1	+225.4	−113.4	−115.9	−132.0	+260.0	+12.1

[a] It should be noted that the official import figures for most countries include the cost of ocean shipping and insurance, while the export figures exclude these charges. This means that net imports are slightly exaggerated, and net exports somewhat understated. See also App. A

That is to say, only 3 are net exporters of both food and raw materials and net importers of manufactured goods. The value of their net exports or net imports—in the aggregate, and for each of these large classes of trade—is given in the table on page 11. All figures are given in dollars, conversions from foreign currencies having been made at current rates of exchange.

Two groups, including 10 states in all, are partially complementary in character to the trade of the old Reich. Six of these countries are net exporters of food and net importers of manufactures. In two classes of commodities, therefore, they dovetail with the German economy. But in raw materials they are like Germany, being, on balance, dependent on outside sources of supply. The trade of these "Group II" countries is summarized in the accompanying table. Figures for Spain are given for 1929, but have not been published for 1937.

GROUP II. EXPORTERS OF FOOD, IMPORTERS OF RAW MATERIALS AND MANUFACTURES, 1937, 1929

[Net imports (+), net exports (−), in millions of dollars][a]

Country	1937				1929			
	Food	Raw Materials	Manu-factures	Total	Food	Raw Materials	Manu-factures	Total
Denmark....	−208.7	+135.2	+ 96.9	+ 23.4	−267.2	+162.2	+130.8	+ 25.8
Hungary.....	− 91.1	+ 58.3	− 0.6	− 33.4	−106.3	+ 58.5	+ 52.2	+ 4.4
Netherlands..	− 78.9	+158.3	+142.2	+221.6	−117.8	+264.7	+159.4	+306.3
Poland.......	− 50.1	+ 33.3	+ 27.9	+ 11.1	− 62.3	− 2.4	+ 98.0	+ 33.3
Portugal.....	− 12.3	+ 31.7	+ 30.7	+ 50.1	+ 1.7	+ 25.5	+ 37.8	+ 65.0
Total......	−441.1	+416.8	+297.1	+272.8	−551.9	+508.5	+478.2	+434.8
Spain........	...	...	...	...	−122.1	+ 79.4	+163.9	+121.2

[a] See note *a* to the table for Group I.

The other four countries make up "Group III." Unlike Germany, they export raw materials and import manufactures. In foodstuffs, however, they are, like Germany, deficit or net-importing countries.

GROUP III. EXPORTERS OF RAW MATERIALS, IMPORTERS OF FOOD AND
MANUFACTURES, 1937, 1929

[Net imports (+), net exports (−), in millions of dollars][a]

Country	1937				1929			
	Food	Raw Materials	Manufactures	Total	Food	Raw Materials	Manufactures	Total
Albania......	0.0	− 1.0	+ 3.7	+ 2.7	+ 0.5	+ 0.4	+ 3.7	+ 4.6
Greece........	+20.6	−18.8	+ 51.7	+ 53.5	+ 38.6	− 19.2	+ 62.4	+ 81.8
Norway......	+ 7.6	−22.1	+131.3	+116.8	+ 8.8	− 25.0	+101.7	+ 85.5
Sweden......	+34.0	−54.9	+ 52.3	+ 31.4	+ 58.3	− 77.9	+ 11.7	− 7.9
Total......	+62.2	−96.8	+239.0	+204.4	+106.2	−121.7	+179.5	+164.0

[a] See note *a* to the table for Group I.

A fourth group includes Germany and the 6 states whose trade is like hers in general outline. These "Group IV" countries contain practically all the great industrial centers of Europe. It will be seen from the accompanying table that for these 7 states combined, net imports of food and net exports of manufactures are roughly twice those for Germany, while net imports of raw materials are almost three times as large. It would seem that expansion over countries like these offers little promise of larger "lebensraum" for the Reich.

GROUP IV. EXPORTERS OF MANUFACTURES, IMPORTERS OF FOOD AND RAW
MATERIALS, 1937, 1929

[Net imports (+), net exports (−), in millions of dollars][a]

Country	1937				1929			
	Food	Raw Materials	Manufactures	Total	Food	Raw Materials	Manufactures	Total
Germany.....	+ 607.4	+ 931.4	−1716.7	−177.9	+ 773.6	+1018.8	−1800.9	− 8.5
Austria......	+ 66.7	+ 48.3	− 70.4	+ 44.6	+ 128.4	+ 69.0	− 46.4	+151.0
Belgium-Luxemburg.	+ 133.5	+ 143.7	− 214.2	+ 63.0	+ 129.6	+ 232.3	− 257.6	+104.3
Czecho-slovakia....	+ 14.8	+ 137.4	− 186.2	− 34.0	+ 44.2	+ 187.8	− 248.1	−16.1
France.......	+ 293.6	+ 723.7	− 272.2	+745.1	+ 276.4	+ 942.5	− 902.4	+316.5
Italy........	− 4.2	+ 348.7	− 165.6	+178.9	+ 62.3	+ 394.6	− 122.2	+334.7
Switzerland...	+ 91.0	+ 104.6	− 77.2	+118.4	+ 96.6	+ 113.7	− 94.7	+115.6
Total......	+1202.8	+2437.8	−2702.5	+938.1	+1511.1	+2958.7	−3472.3	+997.5

[a] See note *a* to the table for Group I.

Taken as a whole, the trade of the enlarged German area is similar in character to that of the old Reich. The area is a net importer of food and raw materials, a net exporter of manufactured goods. In fact, even when absolute amounts are compared, there is no marked difference between the net trade of the old Reich and the larger area now under German domination *except* in the case of raw materials. This is shown by the accompanying summary table and by the figures for Germany given in the table for "Group IV" countries.

SUMMARY FOR ALL STATES OF NAZI EUROPE, 1937, 1929

[Net imports (+), net exports (−), in millions of dollars][a]

Group	1937				1929			
	Food	Raw Materials	Manufactures	Total	Food	Raw Materials	Manufactures	Total
I...........	− 175.7	− 163.1	+ 225.4	− 113.4	− 115.9	− 132.0	+ 260.0	+ 12.1
II...........	− 441.1	+ 416.8	+ 297.1	+ 272.8	− 551.9	+ 508.5	+ 478.2	+ 434.8
III........	+ 62.2	− 96.8	+ 239.0	+ 204.4	+ 106.2	− 121.7	+ 179.5	+ 164.0
IV........	+1202.8	+2437.8	−2702.5	+ 938.1	+1511.1	+2958.7	−3472.3	+ 997.5
Total.....	+ 648.2	+2594.7	−1941.0	+1301.9	+ 949.5	+3213.5	−2554.6	+1608.4

[a] See note *a* to the table for Group I. Spain is not included.

In the case of raw materials, the existing German shortage has actually been greatly increased by the expansion over additional territory. According to the figures for 1937 and 1929, net imports of such commodities for the whole of Nazi Europe are roughly three times as large as for Germany alone. As a result, the close balance existing between all commodity imports and exports in the trade of the old Reich is replaced by a large import balance for the area as a whole.[4] It would seem that a bad situation has been made worse by the measures taken to improve it.

---

[4] The question of how the commodity balance was settled in former years is left to Chap. VI.

How would these conclusions be modified if Mediter-ranean Asia and Africa were included in the area? In the past, this region has been closely associated with Europe. Can it supply the commodities and markets required to balance Europe's trade?

Figures broken down by large commodity classes are available for only five of these political units (Algeria, French Morocco, Tunisia, Egypt, and Turkey), but they cover by far the greater part of the trade under consideration. They are given below, together with the trade of the German area. The figures show net trade (the plus sign indicating net imports and the minus sign net exports), in millions of dollars.

Trade	Nazi Europe	Mediterranean Africa and Asia	Total
1937:			
Food..............	+ 648.2	−124.8	+ 523.4
Raw materials.........	+2,594.7	−197.9	+2,396.8
Manufactures.........	−1,941.0	+311.4	−1,629.6
Total.............	+1,301.9	− 11.3	+1,290.6
1929:			
Food..............	+ 949.5	− 43.3	+ 906.2
Raw materials.........	+3,213.5	−222.7	+2,990.8
Manufactures.........	−2,554.6	+476.1	−2,078.5
Total.............	+1,608.4	+210.1	+1,818.5

These southern Mediterranean countries provide some of the food and raw materials needed by Nazi Europe, and absorb a considerable volume of the manufactures it produces. However, if their whole trade were monopolized by their neighbors to the north, it would not suffice to meet the latter's trade requirements. And, whether they are in or out of the reckoning, the situation portrayed by the figures is much farther out of balance in the case of the larger area now under German control than it was for old Germany alone.[5] That is, larger Germany would have to import more food and raw materials, and find larger markets for manufactures, than were required for the old Reich.

[5] It is sometimes assumed that Germany may move into Soviet Russia and thereby acquire control over large additional productive resources. Without analyzing the trade of Russia in detail, it may be pointed out that her total exports, including all kinds of commodities, amounted to only 332 million dollars in 1937, and to 475 millions in 1929. That is, Russia's *total* exports have amounted to only about one-third of the *net* imports shown for the German area. Trade figures for the U.S.S.R. are given below, in millions of dollars.

Trade	1937			1929		
	Imports	Exports	Net	Imports	Exports	Net
Food.............	25.3	76.2	−50.9	44.3	102.6	− 58.3
Raw materials......	128.5	194.4	−65.9	199.1	297.8	− 98.7
Manufactures.......	103.8	61.4	+42.4	209.7	74.9	+134.8
Total...........	257.6	332.0	−74.4	453.1	475.3	− 22.2

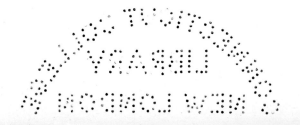

CHAPTER II

SHORTAGES AND EXPORTABLE SUPPLIES OF PRINCIPAL FOODSTUFFS

The world's trade in foodstuffs is largely concerned with a short list of commodities: cereals, meat, vegetable oils and oilseeds, potatoes, dairy products, sugar, fruit, wine, coffee, tea, cacao, and tobacco. In the trade of Nazi Europe, some of these commodities are normally on an import basis, some are produced for export. In the analysis of Chapter I, food exports of all kinds were balanced against food imports to show the money cost of the area's net imports from outside sources. No question was raised there concerning the character of the component goods or the meaning of a figure reached by canceling an export commodity, for example, potatoes, against an import commodity, such as coffee. It is clear, however, that only through foreign trade can an exportable surplus of potatoes provide the coffee that is wanted from outside sources. In the present chapter the food requirements and supplies of the area will be considered in terms of individual commodities, the purpose being to determine in a more concrete way the extent to which the area has been self-sufficient or dependent upon world trade for its food supply.

I. FOODSTUFF SHORTAGES

With production and consumption at customary levels, Nazi Europe has long experienced a shortage in the domestic supply of two large and important classes of necessary foodstuffs—cereals and vegetable oils and oilseeds. There has also been a shortage or complete lack of domestic production in a number of commodities that are sometimes classed as "enjoyment goods"—tobacco, coffee, tea, and cacao. In sugar and fruit the area is an important producer, but increased consumption in recent years has required imports from foreign sources in excess of exports. And, strange as it may seem, the area is also a net importer of wine, for, though it is the world's principal producer of this commodity, it is also the principal consumer.

A. Cereals

For centuries the cereals have been the staple food for civilized man and feed for his flocks and herds. In recent decades their consumption has tended to diminish in many countries, as a wider variety of foods became available to the population at large. However, in 1929 they accounted for 16.2 per cent of world trade in agricultural products, and for 16.9 per cent in 1937.[1]

Net imports of cereals from outside sources account for around 9 to 10 per cent of the quantities consumed in Nazi Europe. While the area is a producer of all the important cereals—wheat, rye, barley, oats, maize, and rice—it is also a net importer in every case. Trade and production figures for the several grains are given on page 19 for the 20 countries combined.

For all of the grains taken together, the excess of imports over exports in 1937 amounted to 11.6 million tons. For 1929 the comparable figure was 14.8 millions. Aggregate consumption—which, aside from unknown changes in the amounts in storage, is measured by production plus net imports—was 130.3 millions in 1937 and 138.0 millions in 1929. In terms of tonnage consumed, the bread grain wheat was by far the most

---

[1] Based on International Institute of Agriculture, *World Trade in Agricultural Products* (1940), p. 510.

important of all, and the feed grain maize was second in importance.

CEREAL TRADE AND PRODUCTION OF NAZI EUROPE, 1937, 1929[a]

(In thousands of metric tons)

Grain	1937[b]			1929		
	Im- ports	Ex- ports	Pro- duction	Im- ports	Ex- ports	Pro- duction
Wheat[c].........	7,026	2,925	40,772	10,870	2,104	37,690
Rye[c]...........	841	591	19,118	921	1,054	22,646
Barley.........	1,357	778	13,884	2,793	1,761	16,022
Oats...........	586	148	20,553	976	715	25,138
Maize..........	6,542	1,559	19,909	5,038	738	17,914
Rice...........	1,742	465	1,119	1,233	613	963
Spelt and meslin.	—	—	3,320	—	—	2,810
Total........	18,094	6,466	118,675	21,831	6,985	123,183

[a] Compiled from International Institute of Agriculture, *International Yearbook of Agricultural Statistics*, 1931–32, and 1938–39.

[b] Including trade for Spain as of 1935, as follows: imports, 53,000 metric tons; exports, 32,000. Later figures for Spain are not available.

[c] Including the flour trade in terms of grain.

All of the states in the area participated in cereal production and trade. As is well known, however, the amounts involved varied widely from country to country, owing to differences in climate, topography, size, and methods of production. The table on page 20 shows net trade, production, and "apparent consumption," by countries. Here, as in Chapter I, the countries are grouped according to the character of their trade.[2]

Only 6 of the 20 countries in the area were net exporters of grain in 1937; only 5 in 1929. This small group was made up of the Balkan countries and Poland. Four countries were net importers of grain although their exports of all foodstuffs combined were greater than their

[2] See pp. 11–13 above.

food imports. These were Denmark and the Netherlands, where the dairy and hog-raising industries provide important exports but call for grain imports, and Spain and Portugal, exporters of fruit and wine. The largest importer, and also the largest producer, was Germany.

THE CEREAL IMPORTING AND EXPORTING STATES OF NAZI
EUROPE 1937, 1929[a]
(In thousands of metric tons)

Countries (By groups)	1937[b]			1929		
	Net Imports (+) Net Exports (−)	Production	Apparent Consumption	Net Imports (+) Net Exports (−)	Production	Apparent Consumption
I. Bulgaria.........	− 332	3,589	3,257	− 57	2,481	2,424
Rumania........	− 2,095	10,393	8,298	− 1,515	13,537	12,022
Yugoslavia.......	− 1,059	8,643	7,584	− 691	7,768	7,077
Total.........	− 3,486	22,625	19,139	− 2,263	23,786	21,523
II. Denmark........	+ 816	3,497	4,313	+ 812	3,503	4,315
Hungary.........	− 730	6,168	5,438	− 1,112	5,735	4,623
Netherlands......	+ 1,857	1,338	3,195	+ 2,364	1,097	3,461
Poland...........	− 315	11,539	11,224	− 379	13,756	13,377
Portugal........	+ 38	1,016	1,054	+ 244	936	1,180
Spain..........	+ 21	8,550	8,571	+ 573	8,546	9,119
Total.........	+ 1,687	32,108	33,795	+ 2,502	33,573	36,075
III. Albania..........	+ 22	206	228	+ 23	...	23 +
Greece..........	+ 603	1,605	2,208	+ 724	706	1,430
Norway..........	+ 546	407	953	+ 482	320	802
Sweden..........	+ 255	3,140	3,395	+ 443	2,937	3,380
Total.........	+ 1,426	5,358	6,784	+ 1,672	3,963	5,635
IV. Germany.........	+ 4,116	22,321	26,437	+ 3,561	22,894	26,455
Austria...........	+ 906	1,859	2,765	+ 858	1,677	2,535
Belgium- Luxemburg.....	+ 2,554	1,488	4,042	+ 2,240	1,848	4,088
Czechoslovakia....	− 94	5,719	5,625	+ 388	6,406	6,794
France..........	+ 2,121	13,724	15,845	+ 2,696	17,399	20,095
Italy.............	+ 1,448	13,192	14,640	+ 2,346	11,382	13,728
Switzerland.......	+ 950	281	1,231	+ 846	255	1,101
Total.........	+12,001	58,584	70,585	+12,935	61,861	74,796
All Nazi Europe.......	+11,628	118,675	130,303	+14,846	123,183	138,029

[a] Compiled from source cited for table on p. 19.
[b] Figures for Spain are for 1935, the latest data available.

The grain trade with countries outside the area has been considerably more important than intra-area trade. An analysis covering more than 97 per cent of the trade shows that the big grain exporters found their principal markets inside the area,[3] but the big importing countries found their principal sources of supply in outside countries. The figures are given in the accompanying table.

WHERE NAZI EUROPE BOUGHT AND SOLD GRAIN, 1937, 1929[a]
(Figures in thousands of metric tons)
I. TRADE IN 1937[b]

Group	Exports to and Imports from Inside the Area			Exports to and Imports from Outside Countries		
	Exports	Imports	Net	Exports	Imports	Net
I...........	3,030	19	−3,011	504	18	− 486
II...........	1,262	542	− 720	363	2,714	+ 2,351
III.........	—	439	+ 439	34	909	+ 875
IV.........	443	3,735	+3,292	768	9,041	+ 8,273
Total.....	4,735	4,735	0	1,669	12,682	+11,013

II. TRADE IN 1929

Group	Exports	Imports	Net	Exports	Imports	Net
I...........	1,315	48	−1,267	1,147	16	− 1,131
II...........	1,453	1,094	− 359	511	3,363	+ 2,852
III.........	87	493	+ 406	8	1,241	+ 1,233
IV.........	1,920	3,140	+1,220	456	12,059	+11,603
Total......	4,775	4,775	0	2,122	16,679	+14,557

[a] Figures showing sources of imports for 1929 are based on the official trade reports of the 20 German-area countries. For 1937, figures for barley, oats, and rye are also from original trade reports, and for other grains from the League of Nations, *International Trade in Certain Raw Materials and Foodstuffs*, 1938. Exports to countries inside the area were compiled from the reports of the importing countries; exports to outside markets were derived by subtracting this intra-area trade from total exports.
[b] Excluding the trade of Spain, for which 1937 data are not available.

Here it is seen that in 1937 the big exporting countries, in Group I, sold more than 85 per cent of their grain to countries now under German domination. The big grain importers, in Group IV, made about 70 per cent of their purchases in outside markets.

[3] This analysis covers imports of 17.4 millions out of a total of 18.1 millions in 1937; and 21.5 out of a total of 21.8 millions in 1929.

The Western Hemisphere has supplied roughly 70 per cent of the grain brought in from outside sources.[4] Argentina alone furnished more than half the total, and Canada more than 10 per cent. Russia, the great grain producer of Europe, furnished less than 4 per cent. In

PRINCIPAL OUTSIDE SOURCES FOR GRAIN, 1937, 1929[a]
(Figures in thousands of metric tons)

Exporting Area	1937			1929		
	Exports to Nazi Europe	Total Exports	Production	Exports to Nazi Europe	Total Exports	Production
Western Hemisphere:						
Argentina...........	6,961	13,851	17,586	7,123	12,711	16,932
Canada.............	1,302	3,461	11,140	3,760	7,413	15,344
United States........	440	2,241	115,118	3,006	5,926	110,626
Chile...............	58	105	1,053	25	110	1,118
Mexico.............	21	22	2,082	20	9	1,915
Brazil..............	...	52	8,067	17	31	6,151
Uruguay............	...	47	423	4	125	427
Seven countries....	8,782	19,779	155,469	13,955	26,325	152,513
Asia and Oceania:						
French Indo-China...	1,452	2,183	6,939	386	1,704	5,886
Australia...........	451	2,793	4,818	392	2,730	4,990
India...............	403	3,801	64,114	487	2,607	64,331
Turkey.............	236	279	7,321	7	14	5,546
Dutch East Indies....	100	251	7,953	142	188	6,794
Siam...............	80	987	3,385	33	1,014	3,917
Iraq...............	35	406	1,330	...	96	...
Iran...............	10	81	3,442	...	68	...
Eight countries....	2,767	10,781	99,302	1,447	8,421	91,464
Africa:						
Egypt.............	71	206	3,809	65	151	3,609
French North Africa[b].	386	440	3,959	835	1,084	4,736
South Africa........	151	803	3,130	108	332	2,074
Portuguese Africa....	61	119	205	58	87	181
Five areas.........	669	1,568	11,103	1,066	1,654	10,600
Soviet Union.........	452	1,355	95,122	5	196	65,209
United Kingdom.......	12	117	4,085	172	405	5,095
Total for all sources listed...............	12,682	33,600	365,081	16,645	37,001	324,881
WORLD TOTAL[c].........	18,094	42,975	521,421	21,831	45,707	484,912

[a] Data for total exports and production are from International Institute of Agriculture, *International Yearbook of Agricultural Statistics,* 1931–32 and 1938–39. Data for exports to Nazi Europe are from the official import figures of the importing countries. See note *a,* table on p. 21.
[b] Including Algeria, Morocco, and Tunisia.
[c] Trade figures include intra-area exports of Nazi Europe, amounting to 4,735,000 metric tons in 1937, and 4,775,000 in 1929

[4] Total imports for the area were 18,094,000 metric tons in 1937, and 21,831,000 in 1929. See table, p. 19 above.

the table on page 22, purchases from the principal outside sources of supply are compared with the total cereal
exports and production of those countries.

From the viewpoint of producing countries outside
the area, the figures suggest that the European market
is a matter of vital importance to some. To others it is of
considerably less concern—except for its effects on their
markets for other types of goods. For example, exports
to the German area accounted for almost 40 per cent of
the grain produced in Argentina; for 20 per cent of that
grown in French Indo-China; but for less than ½ of 1
per cent in the case of the Soviet Union and the United
States.

*By extending control over all of Mediterranean Africa
and Asia, the area would not greatly reduce the volume of
its grain imports*. This is shown by the figures below, in
thousands of metric tons—the plus sign indicating net
imports, and the minus sign net exports.

Territory	1937		1929	
Nazi Europe...............		+11,628		+14,846
Mediterranean Africa:				
Algeria...................	−106		−201	
French Morocco..........	+ 9		−409	
Tunisia..................	− 61		−363	
Egypt....................	−202		+220	
Libya....................	+ 18		+ 59	
Spanish Morocco.........	+ 71		...	
Tangier Zone.............	+ 19	− 252	+ 12	− 682
Mediterranean Asia:				
Turkey...................	−279		+153	
Syria and Lebanon........	+ 18		+ 98	
Palestine................	+113		+ 57	
Cyprus..................	+ 30	− 118	+ 15	+ 323
Total.....................		+11,258		+14,487

It is seen that the exportable supply of cereals, from all of these Mediterranean countries combined, has in recent years amounted to less than 400,000 metric tons. This compares with net imports into Nazi Europe of 11,628,000 metric tons in 1937, and of 14,846,000 in 1929. The table on page 23 gives a summary view of the part the several countries played in the grain trade of the whole Mediterranean area, and also of their un- importance as sources of supply for continental Europe.

The shifts shown by these figures and by the table on page 19 above reflect in part the change from a good crop year in 1929 to a poor year in 1937 throughout the Old World. In part, they resulted from the changing trade and production policies of European governments.

Every effort was made to restrict consumption in 1937—because of the short crop and the difficulties in- volved in financing imports. And to increase readily available supplies of grain, many of the European governments were encouraging increased production, not only at home, but also in trans-Mediterranean areas. The net result, according to the figures for 1937 and 1929 in the table on page 20, was a reduction of 7.7 million tons in "apparent" consumption, and of 3.2 millions in net imports. This, however, undoubtedly exaggerates the extent to which consumption was actually curtailed, since it takes no account of the building up of stores in 1929, nor of their depletion in 1937.

It is not likely that consumption could be held at the low indicated by the production and trade figures for 1937, nor that production could be sustained year after year at the high level shown for 1929. But, even if these conditions could be realized, and if the area were extended across the Mediterranean, there still would be a need for considerable imports of foreign grain.

B. Vegetable Oils

Vegetable oils have an important place in the diet of Europe, and in a number of industries, particularly in soap manufacture. Oilseed cakes, the by-product from the oil mills, are used in the dairy and meat-producing industries. By far the greater part of the oils are consumed in the form of margarine (more than 60 per cent in the case of Germany), salad oil and soap accounting for most of the remainder, except for relatively small amounts used for technical purposes.

In comparison with the total for all fats, the consumption of vegetable oils varies from country to country. In Germany, for example, where the consumption of meat and butter is high, not more than a third of the fats used for all purposes are from oilseeds and fruits, while butter, lard, bacon, and other animal fats account for the rest. In Italy, on the other hand, more than half of the fats consumed are of vegetable origin.[5]

Net imports of oil and oilseeds account for more than 60 per cent of the vegetable oils consumed in Nazi Europe. In fact, the only vegetable oil produced there in appreciable quantities is olive oil, which accounted for 84 per cent of the domestic supply of vegetable oil in 1937, and for 90 per cent in 1929. Trade and production figures for the most important of the oils are given on page 26 for the area as a whole.

[5] The ratios given for Germany are based partly on Karl Brandt, *The German Fat Plan and Its Economic Setting* (1938), pp. 38–39, 52, and on an unpublished study by Werner Baer. For Italy, they are based on an unpublished study by Al Costanzo.

VEGETABLE-OIL TRADE AND PRODUCTION OF NAZI EUROPE, 1937, 1929[a]

(In thousands of metric tons)

Oil	1937[b]		1929	
	Net Imports (+) Net Exports (−)	Production	Net Imports (+) Net Exports (−)	Production
Olive................	− 48	1,008	− 73	1,124
Peanut..............	+551	7	+524	7
Coconut.............	+444	—	+462	—
Palm and palm kernel.	+338	—	+192	—
Linseed.............	+274	56	+298	52
Soybean.............	+207	14	+254	—
Castor..............	+ 34	. . .	+ 28	. . .
Cottonseed	+ 8	13	+ 22	2
Sesame..............	+ 31	6	+ 42	3
Rapeseed............	+ 6	76	+ 18	44
Hempseed...........	. . .	19	. . .	16
Total.............	+1,845	1,199	+1,767	1,248

[a] From International Institute of Agriculture, *International Yearbook of Agricultural Statistics*, 1931–32 and 1938–39; except for castor oil in 1929, which was compiled from the same, *Oils and Fats, Production and International Trade, Part I*. The totals are partially incomplete, since data not available (. . .) are added in as if they were zeros.

The figures include oilseeds and nuts in oil equivalents, based on the following conversion ratios, in percentages: peanuts unshelled 28, shelled 40; linseed 31; copra 62; palm kernels 45; castor beans 40; cottonseed 17; soybeans 17; sesame 51; rapeseed 35.

[b] These figures include the trade and production of Spain as of 1935, since 1937 data are not available.

On balance, olive oil is exported from the area, but in relatively small amounts. For all of the other oils, the area is on an import basis.

Production of vegetable oils in appreciable quantities is limited to 3 of the 20 countries: Spain, Italy, and Greece. All three are primarily producers of olive oil, and of the 3, only Spain exported more than she imported. Three of the Balkan countries were also net exporters of vegetable oils (principally in the form of oilseeds), although their production was on a small scale: Bulgaria, Rumania, and Albania. The trade and production of the

VEGETABLE-OIL TRADE AND PRODUCTION, BY COUNTRIES, 1937, 1929[a]
(In thousands of metric tons, with oilseeds included in terms of oil)

Countries (By groups)	1937[b]		1929	
	Net Imports (+) Net Exports (−)	Production	Net Imports (+) Net Exports (−)	Production
I. Bulgaria..........	− 1.9	9.4	+ 3.9	1.9
Rumania..........	− 5.1	35.3	+ 3.6	18.9
Yugoslavia........	+ 2.2	12.7	+ 12.6	13.8
Total..........	− 4.8	57.4	+ 20.1	34.6
II. Denmark..........	+ 71.9	—	+ 78.1	—
Hungary..........	+ 4.6	4.1	+ 1.8	3.1
Netherlands.......	+ 107.1	5.6	+ 160.2	5.6
Poland............	+ 17.9	47.5	+ 42.5	40.0
Portugal..........	+ 33.1	97.2	+ 3.5	75.8
Spain.............	− 28.1	446.9	− 48.6	668.4
Total..........	+ 206.5	601.3	+ 237.5	792.9
III. Albania..........	− 0.1	—	− 1.7	—
Greece............	+ 0.1	199.0	− 8.5	82.4
Norway...........	+ 40.8	—	+ 44.9	—
Sweden...........	+ 73.2	—	+ 60.6	—
Total..........	+ 114.0	199.0	+ 95.3	82.4
IV. Germany..........	+ 604.4	42.1	+ 713.7	7.5
Austria...........	+ 29.8	1.0	+ 19.8	1.1
Belgium-Luxemburg	+ 92.0	4.2	+ 82.0	5.7
Czechoslovakia.....	+ 78.9	7.1	+ 50.7	4.5
France............	+ 501.7	9.7	+ 419.7	25.7
Italy.............	+ 199.4	277.3	+ 112.6	293.7
Switzerland.......	+ 23.3	—	+ 15.5	—
Total..........	+1,529.5	341.4	+1,414.0	338.2
All Nazi Europe........	+1,845.2	1,199.1	+1,766.9	1,248.1

[a] For sources of data and list of oils included here, see preceding table.
[b] Figures for Spain are for 1935, the latest data available.

20 countries are shown in the accompanying table, with oilseeds included in terms of their oil content.

In vegetable oils, as in the case of cereals, the big importing and consuming countries are Germany and France. Together they have accounted for well over half of the net imports of the whole area and, with other Group IV countries (whose trade was like Germany is), for well over 80 per cent. Countries in Group II (foodstuff exporters) also imported large amounts of vegetable oils. Group I had small net exports in 1937. Consumption was somewhat smaller than is indicated by these figures, particularly for Denmark and the Netherlands, since there was some re-export in the form of margarine, a commodity not included in these figures.[6]

The Far East, tropical Africa, and Argentina have supplied most of the vegetable oils and oilseeds imported from outside the area. The table on page 29 shows the principal sources of supply for vegetable oils, and the principal oil exported from each of the sources listed. The figures given in the table cover the 6 oils and oilseeds of outstanding importance in the external trade of the area—peanut, coconut, palm and palm kernel, soybean, linseed, and castor bean. In the aggregate, these oils (and seeds) accounted for total imports of 2,252,000 metric tons of oil in 1937 out of a total of 2,390,000 tons for the 10 oils included in the trade table on page 26 above.

Peanuts came principally from India and tropical Africa; coconuts and copra from the Dutch East Indies, British Malaya, and nearby territories; linseed from Argentina; palm kernels from tropical Africa; soybeans from China; and castor beans from Brazil. In large part these imports were in the form of nuts and seeds—to be crushed in European mills, where they provided on the

---

[6] Margarine exports from the Netherlands amounted to 11,000 metric tons in 1937, and to 72,000 in 1929.

average about one-third their weight in oil, and two-thirds in oilseed cakes.

PRINCIPAL SOURCES SUPPLYING OIL AND OILSEEDS, 1937, 1929[a]

(Figures show oil, or oil content of seeds, in thousands of metric tons)

Exporting Area	Principal Oil	Exports to Nazi Europe			
		1937		1929	
Asia and Oceania:					
India..............	Peanut	312		546	
Dutch East Indies...	Coconut	284		280	
China..............	Soybean	207		240	
British Malaya......	Coconut	81		35	
Oceania............	Coconut	66		43	
Philippine Islands....	Coconut	8		28	
French Indo-China...	Coconut	7		9	
Japan..............	Soybean	1	966	33	1,214
Africa:					
French Tropical.....	Peanut and palm	289		138	
British Tropical.....	Palm and peanut	245		213	
Belgian Congo......	Palm	73		48	
Portuguese colonies..	Peanut	20		8	
Others[b]............	Coconut	53	680	14	421
Western Hemisphere:					
Argentina...........	Linseed	311		306	
Brazil..............	Castor	16		4	
Uruguay............	Linseed	3		—	
Canada............	Soybean	2		—	
United States.......	Linseed	—	332	2	312
Other Europe:					
Great Britain.......	Imported soybean, palm, and coconut	69		51	
Lithuania and Latvia.	Linseed	4		7	
Russia.............	Soybean and castor	—	73	7	65
Total for sources listed.	6 oils		2,051		2,012
Total imports into Nazi Europe (10 oils).......			2,390		2,468

[a] Figures for all six oils in 1929, and for palm and palm kernel, soybean, linseed, and castor oils in 1937 were compiled from import statistics by country of origin as reported in the official trade volumes of the 20 countries in the area. Figures for 1937 for peanut and coconut oils were compiled from League of Nations, *International Trade in Certain Raw Materials and Foodstuffs*, 1938.

[b] All of these amounts were identified as coming from Africa, most of them from tropical regions.

In value terms, the imports of all vegetable oils and seeds accounted for 16 per cent of the total food imports of the area,[7] and for 4.5 per cent of all imports. From the point of view of foreign exporters of oils and oilseeds, the amounts sent to Nazi Europe were of sizeable proportions. For India, they represented 5 per cent of the value of total exports of all kinds; for Argentina, 7 per cent; and for Netherlands East Indies, 6 per cent.

The Mediterranean sections of Asia and Africa are not important exporters of vegetable oils and seeds. The figures given below show the net trade of these countries, together with that of Nazi Europe as a whole. They are in thousands of metric tons, with the plus sign indicating net imports, and the minus sign net exports.

Territory	1937		1929	
Nazi Europe............		+1,845.2		+1,766.9
Mediterranean Africa:				
Algeria..............	+27.1		+ 9.9	
French Morocco.......	+ 2.5		− 4.8	
Tunisia..............	− 6.1		−40.3	
Egypt...............	−43.1		−56.6	
Libya...............	+ 1.4		+ 1.4	
Spanish Morocco......	+ 5.8		...	
Tangier Zone.........	+ 1.1	− 11.3	+ 0.1	− 90.3
Mediterranean Asia:				
Turkey..............	− 3.9		−10.8	
Syria and Lebanon.....	− 2.1		− 1.5	
Palestine............	+ 5.8		+ 2.5	
Cyprus..............	− 0.2	− 0.4	...	− 9.8
Total.................		+1,833.5		+1,666.8

[7] In the Brussels classification, oilseeds, oil fruits, oilcakes, and tobacco are included with raw materials. For purposes of the comparison above, the value of the foods group given on p. 14 has been adjusted to include these items.

Cottonseed comes from Egypt and some olive oil from Algeria, French Morocco, Tunisia, and Syria and Lebanon. However, the quantities are not large and there are small offsetting net imports of other vegetable oils.

Only a very small reduction in the import requirements for vegetable oils would result from bringing these Mediterranean countries inside the German area. More than half of consumptive demand would still have to be supplied from outside sources.

C. Some "Necessary" Luxuries

Coffee, cacao, tea, and tobacco are sometimes classed as "enjoyment goods." From a nutritional point of view, all of them, with the exception of cacao, might well be omitted from the foods category. All of them, however, with the possible exception of cacao, would certainly appear among the necessaries budgeted for American families at all income levels. In terms of the quantities entering world trade, coffee is by far the most important of the group—world exports of coffee amounting to a little less than 1.5 million metric tons in 1929, and a little more in 1937. This was from 2½ to 4 times world exports of any of the other three commodities considered here.

All of the coffee, cacao, and tea, and more than one-third of the tobacco consumed in Nazi Europe are imported from outside sources. Of coffee, cacao, and tobacco the amounts consumed there usually bulk large when compared with world production or with the amounts entering world trade. But tea consumption in Nazi Europe has been of decidedly small proportions, accounting for only 5 per cent of world production or of world exports in 1937. The table on page 32 shows net trade in these commodities, and tobacco production, in 1929 and 1937.

CURRENT SUPPLIES OF FOUR "NECESSARY" LUXURIES, 1937, 1929[a]

(In thousands of metric tons)

Countries (By groups)	1937[b]					1929				
	Net Imports (+) Net Exports (−)				Production of Tobacco	Net Imports (+) Net Exports (−)				Production of Tobacco
	Coffee	Cacao	Tea	Tobacco		Coffee	Cacao	Tea	Tobacco	
I. Bulgaria......	+ 1	+ 1	—	− 22	35	+ 1	—	+ .1	− 20	33
Rumania.....	+ 3	+ 2	+ .3	—	10	+ 4	+ 2	+ .6	...	26
Yugoslavia...	+ 7	+ 1	+ .2	− 4	21	+ 10	+ 1	+ .4	− 3	14
Total......	+ 11	+ 4	+ .5	− 26	66	+ 15	+ 3	+ 1.1	− 23	73
II. Denmark.....	+ 27	+ 4	+ .5	+ 8	—	+ 25	+ 3	+ .6	+ 6	—
Hungary.....	+ 2	+ 3	+ .2	− 7	20	+ 4	+ 2	+ .4	− 11	30
Netherlands..	+ 36	+ 53	+11.9	+ 30	—	+ 34	+ 50	+13.0	+ 32	—
Poland.......	+ 6	+ 7	+ 1.9	+ 8	14	+ 8	+ 5	+ 2.1	+ 16	9
Portugal.....	+ 5	—	+ .2	+ 3	—	+ 4	+ 1	+ .3	+ 4	—
Spain........	+ 24	+ 10	+ .1	+ 27	7	+ 24	+ 9	+ .2	+ 31	5
Total......	+100	+ 77	+14.8	+ 69	41	+ 99	+ 70	+16.6	+ 78	44
III. Albania	+ 1	—	—	—	2	+ 1	—	—	...	—
Greece.......	+ 5	+ 2	+ .1	− 42	69	+ 6	+ 1	+ .3	− 50	69
Norway......	+ 17	+ 3	+ .2	+ 3	—	+ 15	+ 2	+ .2	+ 2	—
Sweden......	+ 47	+ 6	+ .4	+ 7	1	+ 41	+ 4	+ .4	+ 8	1
Total......	+ 70	+ 11	+ .7	− 32	72	+ 63	+ 7	+ .9	− 40	70
IV. Germany.....	+178	+ 72	+ 5.0	+ 97	33	+148	+ 80	+ 5.8	+103	23
Austria.......	+ 5	+ 5	+ .3	+ 8	—	+ 9	+ 6	+ .6	+ 12	—
Belgium-Luxemburg.	+ 49	+ 10	+ .3	+ 18	6	+ 38	+ 8	+ .3	+ 22	7
Czechoslovakia	+ 11	+ 10	+ .5	+ 9	14	+ 13	+ 8	+ .7	+ 21	9
France.......	+185	+ 41	+ 1.4	+ 26	31	+170	+ 36	+ 1.6	+ 39	29
Italy........	+ 38	+ 8	+ .1	− 5	43	+ 47	+ 7	+ .2	+ 3	48
Switzerland...	+ 13	+ 7	+ .8	+ 7	1	+ 13	+ 9	+ .7	+ 7	1
Total......	+479	+153	+ 8.4	+160	128	+438	+154	+ 9.9	+207	117
All Nazi Europe...	+660	+245	+24.4	+171	307	+615	+234	+28.5	+222	304

[a] Compiled from International Institute of Agriculture, *International Yearbook of Agricultural Statistics*, 1931–32 and 1938–39, except for tobacco trade in 1929, which was compiled from the following sources: Portugal, exports assumed to be zero, imports from U. S. Dept. of Commerce, *Commerce Yearbook, 1931, Vol. II, Foreign Countries*, p. 218; Turkey, from U. S. Dept. of Agriculture, *Annual Report on Tobacco Statistics*, 1937, p. 100; other countries, from the same, *Yearbook of Agriculture*, 1933.
[b] Data for Spain are for 1935, the latest available.

France has been the area's principal importer of coffee. In fact, she was second largest in the world in 1937, her imports being surpassed only by those of the United States. On a per capita basis, however, some of the Baltic countries were in first rank, consuming more than either France or the United States. In cacao Germany was the largest importer in the area. In tea the Netherlands stood first, accounting for almost one-half the net imports of the whole area.[8] Greece was the largest producer of tobacco and Germany the largest importer and consumer.

Imports of "necessary" luxuries have come in from all parts of the world. Coffee comes principally from South America, cacao from tropical Africa, tea from the Dutch East Indies, and tobacco in almost equal quantities from the United States and the Dutch East Indies.

The accompanying table shows the principal sources from which the first three of these commodities have been procured. It also shows how the area's purchases compared with aggregate production in the countries of supply. Tobacco, a commodity supplied partly from domestic, partly from outside, sources is considered on page 35 below.

PRINCIPAL SOURCES OF CACAO, TEA, AND COFFEE, 1937, 1929[a]

(Figures are in thousands of metric tons)

I. CACAO

Exporting Country	1937		1929	
	Exports to Nazi Europe	Total Ex-ports	Exports to Nazi Europe	Total Ex-ports
Africa:				
British[b]......	136	354	109	304
French West [b]	44	83	26	32
Portuguese...	5	9	6	19
Spanish......	...	6	7	9
South America:				
Ecuador.....	14	19	5	18
Brazil.......	12	105	19	66
Venezuela....	5	16	6	21
Total..........	216	592	178	469
WORLD TOTALS..	235[c]	670	232[c]	576

II. TEA, 1937

Exporting Country	Exports to Nazi Europe	Total Exports	Pro-duction
Dutch East Indies......	13	68	75
India and Ceylon.....	9	266	292
China........	2	41	...
French Indo-China......	.6	2	11
Japan........	.3	35	67
Total........	25	412	445
WORLD TOTALS.	25	449	465

[a] Trade data for 1937 are from League of Nations, *International Trade in Certain Raw Materials and Foodstuffs*, 1938. Exports to Nazi Europe for 1929 were compiled from the official trade statistics of the importing countries. Production data and total exports for 1929 and world total exports are from International Institute of Agriculture, *International Yearbook of Agricultural Statistics*, 1931–32 and 1938–39. Production data available for cacao are altogether unsatisfactory. In cases where coffee production figures were unavailable or appeared to be incomplete, total exports are shown.

[8] Britain, with four of her dominions, usually takes two-thirds of the world's tea imports, while India and Ceylon account for approximately two-thirds of the exports.

III. COFFEE

Exporting Country	1937			1929		
	Exports to Nazi Europe	Total Exports	Production	Exports to Nazi Europe	Total Exports	Production
South America:						
Brazil[d].........	264	727	1546	305	857	1577
Colombia........	57	248	268	12	170	170
Venezuela........	35	42	60	32	64	64
Ecuador.........	8	14	14	5	7	7
Four countries...	364	1031	1888	354	1098	1818
Other Latin America:						
Guatemala.......	24	47	57	34	44	44
Salvador.........	23	68	68	21	47	65
Haiti............	19	25	25	21	29	29
Mexico..........	15	35	40	12	30	39
Costa Rica.......	14	27	27	...	20	20
Five countries...	95	202	217	88	170	197
Asia:						
Dutch East Indies..	59	101	132	54	81	114
British India......	7	7	17	5	5	18
Two countries...	66	108	149	59	86	132
Africa:						
Madagascar.......	25	21	22	3	4	4
Belgian Congo.....	18	18	20	1	1	2
Two countries...	43	39	42	4	5	6
Total for sources listed	568	1380	2296	505	1359	2153
WORLD TOTALS.......	636[e]	1547	2488	615[e]	1475	2497

[b] These figures include British Togo and Cameroons, and French Togo and Cameroons, respectively. Aggregate exports from other French Africa and Madagascar were negligible in 1929 and only 1,400 tons in 1937.
[e] These figures represent total net imports into Nazi Europe from all sources. Aggregate imports are slightly higher owing to intra-area trade (re-exports).
[d] In 1937 Brazil destroyed 1,032,000 metric tons, and consumed 396,000—part of it from stocks on hand at the beginning of the year. In 1929 Brazilian consumption was 228,000 tons and no destruction was reported. (See p. 1015 of *International Yearbook of Agricultural Statistics*, 1938–39.)

Data covering 96 per cent of the area's tobacco trade for 1937 show that the producing countries found their principal markets in the large industrial countries of Europe. The latter, however, supplemented these purchases by even larger imports from outside sources. The table on page 35 analyzes the trade to show the general location of markets and sources.

WHERE NAZI EUROPE BOUGHT AND SOLD TOBACCO, 1937[a]
(Figures in thousands of metric tons)

Group	Exports to and Imports from Inside the Area			Exports to and Imports from Outside the Area		
	Exports	Imports	Net	Exports	Imports	Net
I............	23	—	−23	3	—	− 3
II...........	8	8	0	3	69	+.66
III..........	30	2	−28	12	8	− 4
IV...........	4	55	+51	3	106	+103
Total......	65	65	0	21	183	+162

[a] This table is similar to the one on p. 21 above (and is from sources listed there for 1937) except that these tobacco data include the trade for Spain as of 1935—since Spain is one of the area's principal tobacco importers, and the 1935 data are the latest available.

The figures below (in thousands of metric tons) show the quantity of tobacco brought from principal outside sources in 1937.[9] According to this table, one-third of the

Outside Sources	Exports to Nazi Europe	Total Exports	Production
Western Hemisphere:			
United States.............	49	197	704
Brazil....................	26	37	93
Cuba....................	5	12	25
Dominican Republic.......	4	3	3
Paraguay.................	2	2	9
Colombia................	1	2	15
Six countries...........	87	253	849
Dutch East Indies...........	50	50	54
Turkey....................	19	22	35
Algeria....................	10	11	18
Madagascar................	4	2	6
Total for sources listed.......	170	338	962
WORLD TOTAL..............	257	547	2,154

[9] The data cover leaf, stem, and leaf-waste tobacco. Trade data are from League of Nations, *International Trade in Certain Raw Materials and Food-*

tobacco imported from outside sources came from the Western Hemisphere. As indicated above, supplies from the Dutch East Indies were also important, and something like 10 per cent of the total came from Africa.

It will be seen that in tobacco the trade of Nazi Europe was of decided importance to the principal supplying countries—accounting for roughly one-half of the exports from that group, and for 18 per cent of their reported production.

With the Nazi area expanded into Mediterranean Africa and Asia, larger imports of coffee, tea, and cacao would be required, but decreased imports of tobacco. These Mediterranean countries, like those of Europe, must import all of the coffee, tea, and cacao they consume. In the case of tobacco, however, production is large enough to provide an exportable supply in excess of consumption. The table on page 37—covering the trade in coffee, tea, and tobacco in 1937 and 1929—gives the net trade of the several Mediterranean countries, and also that for Nazi Europe. Since negligible imports of cacao are reported for these Mediterranean countries, they are omitted from the table.

At the levels of production and consumption obtaining in 1937 and 1929, the inclusion of these Mediterranean countries would involve an increase of 5 per cent in net imports of coffee, and of 60 to 90 per cent in the

---

stuffs, 1938; production data, from International Institute of Agriculture, *International Yearbook of Agricultural Statistics*, 1938–39, except the estimate for Paraguay, which is from the U. S. Dept. of Commerce, *Foreign Commerce Yearbook*, 1938, p. 269.

Complete data for total exports from Paraguay are not available. The "world total" given in the first two columns includes intra-area trade of Nazi Europe; and in the last column, excludes production of the U.S.S.R.

"Necessary" Luxury Imports of Nazi Europe and Mediterranean
Areas, 1937, 1929[a]

(Net imports, in thousands of metric tons)

Territory	1937			1929		
	Coffee	Tea	Tobacco[b]	Coffee	Tea	Tobacco[b]
Mediterranean Africa:						
Algeria...........	14.6	1.5	− 6.8	12.0	1.2	−10.6
French Morocco...	2.5	8.1	1.7	1.8	7.1	...
Tunisia...........	1.5	1.8	1.1	1.6	1.4	1.0
Egypt............	7.9	7.3	6.0	9.5	5.8	7.2
Libya............	.7	1.9	.1[c]	.4	1.1	.4
Spanish Morocco	.4	.6	—	...	—	—
Tangier Zone......	.1	.1	—	.2	.2	...
Mediterranean Asia:						
Turkey...........	5.0	1.0	−39.0	6.0	1.0	−33.0
Syria and Lebanon.	1.2	.2	− 1.0	.1	.2	1.4
Palestine.........	1.8	.3	.2	.1	.1	.1
Cyprus...........	.4	—	.2	—	—	.2
Total, Mediterranean	36.1	22.8	−37.5	31.7	18.1	−33.3
Nazi Europe........	636	24.3	171	615	28.5	222
Total............	672.1	47.1	133.5	646.7	46.6	188.7

[a] From sources indicated by footnotes to earlier tables. Cacao is omitted
here, since in 1929 no cacao imports were reported for this Mediterranean
area; and in 1937, a total of less than 1,000 tons was shown for the 4
countries reporting imports.
[b] Minus sign indicates net exports.
[c] Figure for 1936.

case of tea; but a decrease of some 22 per cent in net
imports of tobacco. For none of these commodities,
however, is self-sufficiency indicated, either for the
larger or the smaller area.

D. Sugar, Fruit, and Wine

Sugar in recent decades has become one of the cheap-
est of the energy-producing foods. Accordingly, there
has been a great increase in its consumption in Europe,
particularly among the poorer sections of the popula-

tion. This has been accompanied by increased consumption of fruits—which is fortunate from a dietary standpoint, since fruits supply many food elements that are altogether lacking in refined sugar. Wine, the ancient form in which great quantities of fruit still are consumed, is an important item in the diet of all income classes in many European countries.

Nazi Europe's production of sugar, fruit, and wine almost equals the amount she consumes. In sugar the area has accounted for roughly 22 to 25 per cent of world production; and has had relatively small export balances in some years, small net imports in others. In wine, production amounted to 87 per cent of the world total in 1929, and 77 per cent in 1937; while net imports amounted to an additional 4 per cent of world production in 1929, and 5 per cent in 1937. In raisins, 1937 production amounted to 33 per cent of the world total; in grapes (not used for wine or raisins), to 50 per cent; and in citrus fruits, to 20 per cent. For these fruits, the area is on an export basis. Dates and bananas, which are not grown in Europe, are imported in considerable quantities. Apples, although domestically produced, are also on an import basis.

The accompanying table, and the one on page 40, give available trade and production data for these commodities, by countries, for 1937 and 1929.

The figures for fruit cover only raisins, grapes not used for wine or raisins, citrus fruits, and bananas. If apples and dates are also included, the net import total for 1937 is increased by 155,000 metric tons, and the net figure for 1929 probably changes from an export to an import total—we do not have precise data on this point.[10]

---

[10] World production data for raisins, grapes, and citrus fruits, and trade figures for apples and dates, are not available for 1929.

CURRENT SUPPLIES OF SUGAR, FRUIT, AND WINE, 1937, 1929[a]
[Sugar and fruit in thousands of metric tons, wine in thousands of hectoliters;
net imports (+), net exports (−)]

Countries (By groups)	1937 Sugar[b] Trade	1937 Sugar[b] Production	1937 Fruit[c] Trade	1937 Wine Trade	1937 Wine Production	1929 Sugar[b] Trade	1929 Sugar[b] Production	1929 Fruit[c] Trade	1929 Wine Trade	1929 Wine Production
I. Bulgaria	+ 3	28	− 33	—	1,446	—	36	—	− 4	1,634
Rumania....	—	70	+ 14	− 2	10,663	− 9	80	+ 15	− 3	5,046
Yugoslavia..	—	34	+ 11	− 16	2,903	− 10	119	+ 10	− 55	2,910
Total.....	+ 3	132	− 8	− 18	15,012	− 19	235	+ 25	− 62	9,590
II. Denmark....	− 23	215	+ 18	+ 58	—	+ 38	122	+ 21	+ 54	—
Hungary....	− 24	111	+ 6	+ 383	4,200	−120	222	+ 10	− 313	2,490
Netherlands.	+ 88	222	+124	+ 103	—	+ 60	238	+ 92	+ 143	—
Poland......	− 52	505	+ 47	+ 27	—	−288	824	+ 21	+ 48	—
Portugal....	+ 69	—	− 3	− 798	8,162	+ 71	—	− 4	− 941	6,671
Spain.......	—d	164	−744d	− 1,317d	17,200	+ 1	237	−865	− 3,782	24,998
Total.....	+ 58	1,217	−552	− 2,310	29,562	−238	1,643	−725	− 4,794	34,159
III. Albania.....	+ 4	—	—	—	—	+ 5	—	—	+ 1	—
Greece......	+ 75	—	−134	− 461	3,730	+ 62	—	− 86	− 1,390	2,546
Norway.....	+ 91	—	+ 34	+ 52	—	+ 76	—	+ 27	+ 49	—
Sweden.....	+ 6	312	+ 62	+ 56	—	+144	110	+ 34	+ 59	—
Total.....	+176	312	− 38	− 353	3,730	+287	110	− 25	− 1,281	2,546
IV. Germany....	+ 7	1,990	+412	+ 927	2,350	−192	1,786	+523	+ 1,108	2,019
Austria......	+ 1	140	+ 40	+ 58	853	+111	106	+ 47	+ 424	573
Belgium-Luxemburg	+ 55	216	+101	+ 406	54	− 36	226	+ 60	+ 428	111
Czechoslovakia...	−259	680	+ 48	+ 83	545	−540	909	+ 39	+ 292	224
France......	+186	872	+441	+11,626	54,331	+209	825	+243	+11,018	65,016
Italy........	− 9	321	−368	− 1,861	34,001	+ 13	405	−348	− 923	41,050
Switzerland..	+144	11	+ 56	+ 916	469	+148	6	+ 40	+ 1,167	800
Total.....	+125	4,230	+730	+12,155	92,603	−287	4,263	+604	+13,514	109,793
All Nazi Europe..	+362	5,891	+132	+ 9,474	140,907	−257	6,251	−121	+ 7,377	156,088
WORLD PRODUCTION....	27,430		—	184,000		25,556		—	179,000	

[a] Data for trade and for wine production are compiled from International Institute of Agriculture, *International Yearbook of Agricultural Statistics*, 1931–32 and 1938–39. Sugar production data are from League of Nations, *Statistical Year-book*, 1938–39, originally compiled by International Institute of Agriculture.
[b] Trade data for sugar include both raw and refined without adjustment; but production figures are in terms of refined sugar, and are for crop years 1937–38 and 1929–30.
[c] Figures include only raisins, grapes (not used for wine or raisins), citrus fruits, and bananas; production data for 1937 are given on p. 40.
[d] For Spain, trade data are for 1935, the latest data available; but production figures are 1937 estimates.

Obviously, the figures give an incomplete picture of fruit consumption, since they omit many native fruits and exclude trade in canned and preserved fruits. Fruit production (for items covered by the trade figures) is shown below for 1937—in thousands of metric tons. Bananas are not listed, since they are not produced in the area.[11]

Producing Country	Grapes[12]	Raisins	Citrus Fruits
I. Bulgaria	102	—	—
Rumania	319	—	—
Yugoslavia	—	—	1
Total	421	—	1
II. Hungary	22	—	—
Netherlands	22	—	—
Spain (1935)	157	18	961
Total	201	18	961
III. Albania	12	—	—
Greece	74	189	39
Total	86	189	39
IV. Germany	1	—	—
Belgium-Luxemburg	12	—	—
Czechoslovakia	11	—	—
France	159	—	2
Italy	109	1	699
Total	292	1	701
All Nazi Europe	1,000	208	1,702

The table on page 39 shows that Germany was by far the largest sugar producer in the area, and in some years also a net importer. Of the other principal producers, Poland and Czechoslovakia were on an export basis; France was a net importer. Four countries—

[11] Compiled from International Institute of Agriculture, *International Yearbook of Agricultural Statistics*, 1938–39. Data are not given here for 1929, since they appear to be much less satisfactory than those available for 1937.
[12] Excluding grapes for wine and raisins.

Portugal, Greece, Norway, and Switzerland—had little
if any domestic supply.

The big wine producer, and importer, was France.
Italy and Spain, also large producers, were on an export
basis.

In fruits, so far as those listed are concerned, Germany
was the principal importer. Spain, Italy, and
Greece were the principal producers and exporters.

*In recent years sugar imports from outside sources have
been maintained at pre-depression levels.* An analysis
covering 99 per cent of the total trade shows that imports
from outside sources were somewhat larger in 1937
than in 1929. Meantime, exports to outside markets
were greatly reduced. On balance, consumption has increased.

WHERE NAZI EUROPE BOUGHT AND SOLD SUGAR 1937, 1929[a]
(Figures in thousands of metric tons)

I. TRADE IN 1937

Group	Exports to and Imports from Inside the Area			Exports to and Imports from Outside Countries		
	Exports	Imports	Net	Exports	Imports	Net
I........	—	—	—	—	—	—
II.......	95	4	− 91	75	221	+146
III.......	—	111	+111	—	70	+ 70
IV.......	166	146	− 20	394	533	+139
Total...	261	261	0	469	824	+355

II. TRADE IN 1929

Group	Exports to and Imports from Inside the Area			Exports to and Imports from Outside Countries		
	Exports	Imports	Net	Exports	Imports	Net
I........	2	2	—	21	—	− 21
II.......	133	76	− 57	399	217	−182
III.......	—	171	+171	1	111	+110
IV.......	533	419	−114	654	478	−176
Total...	668	668	0	1,075	806	−269

[a] For sources of data see footnote *a*, table on p. 39.

The Western Hemisphere was the most important out-side source for sugar. Appreciable amounts were also supplied from the Dutch East Indies and Africa, and by the re-export trade from Britain. This is shown by the table below—which also gives the total exports and production of the exporting countries. It will be seen that in 1937 Nazi Europe took approximately 10 per cent of the crop grown by the four principal sugar producers of the Western Hemisphere, and 70 per cent of that for Africa.

PRINCIPAL OUTSIDE SOURCES FOR SUGAR, 1937, 1929[a]
(Figures in thousands of metric tons)

Exporting Country	1937			1929		
	Exports to Nazi Europe	Total Exports	Pro-duction	Exports to Nazi Europe	Total Exports	Pro-duction
Western Hemisphere:						
Cuba..............	143	2,667	2,870	287	5,029	4,440
Dominican Republic.	126	430	400	45	321	340
French West Indies..	105	107	110	29	36	64
Peru..............	10	312	343	26	363	400
Four countries.....	384	3,516	3,723	387	5,749	5,244
Dutch East Indies.....	112	1,138	1,399	197	2,432	2,916
Africa:						
Reunion............	88	88	80	26 {	38	51
Madagascar........	10	9	11		5	5
Portuguese colonies..	68	100	148	57	101	96
Belgian Congo.......	10	12	15	—	—	1
Four countries.....	176	209	254	83	144	153
United Kingdom.......	109	331	383	102	169	293
Russia..............	29	134	2,400	—	127	958
Total for sources listed	810	5,328	8,159	769	8,621	9,564
WORLD TOTAL[b]........	1,092	11,906	27,430	1,486	14,585	25,556

[a] Exports to Nazi Europe in 1929 were compiled from official trade statistics of the importing countries; and for 1937, from League of Nations,

The trade in wine and fruit has been principally intra-area in character. Spain, the principal fruit exporter, made her largest sales in Great Britain, but France and Germany were also important customers. Italy, ranking second among the fruit exporters, sold about one-third of her exports in Germany—both in 1937 and 1929—and roughly 12 per cent in Great Britain, her market of next importance.

Germany, the principal fruit importer in the area, obtained roughly 25 per cent of her imports from Italy. In 1929 she also bought considerable amounts in Spain and the United States, but shifted to the Balkan countries in 1937, greatly curtailing her purchases in Spain, and practically eliminating those in the United States. France, the second largest importer, went to Spain for more than 45 per cent of her imports in 1929, with the United States and Algeria also important sources of supply. In 1937, with the Spanish supply greatly reduced, France bought 35 per cent of her imports in her own colonies—principally in Algeria—and increased her purchases in the United States and Italy.

By far the largest international trader in wine, and also the largest consumer, was France—importer of tremendous quantities of the cheaper wines from Algeria, and exporter to outside markets of smaller amounts of the high-grade varieties. Her principal markets in 1929 were Great Britain, Belgium, and Germany; in

---

International Trade in Certain Raw Materials and Foodstuffs, 1938. Total exports were compiled from the International Institute of Agriculture, *International Yearbook of Agricultural Statistics,* 1931–32 and 1938–39. Production data are from League of Nations, *Statistical Year-book,* 1938–39.

Production data are in terms of refined sugar, while the trade data include both raw and refined without adjustment. This accounts in part for the excess of exports over production in certain cases.

b Trade figures include intra-area trade of Nazi Europe amounting to 251,000 tons in 1937 and 668,000 tons in 1929.

1937, Great Britain, the United States, and Belgium. Spain, the largest wine exporter, sold roughly two-thirds of her exports in France in 1929. During the thirties, however, when France was encouraging increased imports from her colonies, efforts were made to expand sales in other markets. By 1935 Switzerland was taking almost one-third of the reduced volume of Spanish exports, while Germany and Great Britain, the markets of second and third importance, together accounted for another one-third.

Italy sold about one-third of her wines in Switzerland, both in 1937 and 1929. Brazil was her second best customer in 1929, but in 1937 was superseded and far outranked by Germany, whose purchases in Italy accounted for about 27 per cent of Italian exports of wine and for about 45 per cent of her own imports.

If the area included Mediterranean Africa and Asia, it would have net exports of wine and of some fruits, but increased net imports of sugar. During the 1930's wine production and exports were greatly increased in the French colonies, in line with policies adopted by the government of France. But even in 1929—as well as in 1937—Algeria was the outstanding wine producer and exporter among these Mediterranean countries, with Tunisia a poor second but much more important than any of the rest. Citrus fruits and grapes are grown in all of the countries bordering on the Mediterranean. However, the trade is relatively small except for the citrus fruit exports from Palestine, recently expanded in response to encouragement from Britain, and the smaller exports from Algeria. All parts of Mediterranean Africa and Asia are on an import basis for sugar, including Egypt, the only sugar producer in this area.

The table given below shows the net trade in sugar, a small group of fruits, and wine, for the Mediterranean area alone, and in combination with Nazi Europe.

TRADE OF THE MEDITERRANEAN AREA, IN SUGAR, FRUIT, AND WINE 1937, 1929[a]

[Sugar and fruit in thousands of metric tons, wine in thousands of hectoliters; net imports (+), net exports (−)]

Territory	1937			1929		
	Sugar	Fruit[b]	Wine	Sugar	Fruit[b]	Wine
Mediterranean Africa:						
Algeria...........	+ 76	− 66	−12,263	+ 76	− 20	−9,239
French Morocco...	+168	− 8	− 37	+131	+ 3	+ 225
Tunisia...........	+ 33	− 6	− 1,089	+ 34	+ 2	− 516
Egypt............	+ 45	—	+ 67	+ 98	+ 27	+ 190
Libya............	+ 9	+ 1	+ 73	+ 9	—	+ 42
Spanish Morocco..	+ 30	—	+ 54	...	...	...
Tangier Zone......	+ 3	+ 1	+ 5	+ 2	—	+ 9
Mediterranean Asia:						
Turkey...........	+ 12	− 29	—	+ 69	− 46	+ 2
Syria and Lebanon.	+ 34	− 12	+ 3	+ 34	− 11	+ 9
Palestine.........	+ 24	−401	− 6	+ 10	− 62	− 9
Cyprus...........	+ 3	− 17	− 73	+ 3	− 10	− 69
Total, Mediterranean	+437	−537	−13,266	+466	−117	−9,356
Nazi Europe........	+362	+132	+ 9,474	−257	−121	+7,377
Total..............	+799	−405	− 3,792	+209	−238	−1,979

[a] Compiled from sources listed in footnote *a*, p. 39.
[b] Including only raisins, grapes (not used for wine or raisins), citrus fruits, and bananas.

This table shows that if the German area were enlarged to take in these Mediterranean countries, it would have an exportable supply of wine amounting to several million hectoliters. The table also indicates net exports of fruit, if only citrus fruits, grapes, raisins, and bananas are considered. However, the 1937 figures show

that net imports of fresh apples and dates into Mediterranean Asia and Africa amounted to 37,000 metric tons
—in addition to the 155,000 into Nazi Europe. Therefore, with fresh apples and dates in the accounting,
the 1937 figure for net exports would be reduced from
405,000 metric tons to 213,000. This would be further
reduced if prunes and other dried and canned fruits
were also considered. For sugar, the figures show that in
1929 and 1937 the larger area—of Nazi Europe and the
Mediterranean area—was on an import basis. Net imports accounted for 3 per cent of consumption in 1929,
and for 12 per cent in 1937. It is of course possible that
storage supplies were being increased in 1937, and therefore that the margin between production and consumption is somewhat narrower than is indicated by the
trade and production figures for that year. But in any
case, the figures indicate that the sugar production of
Nazi Europe is inadequate, if consumption is to be
maintained at the levels of recent years.

II. EXPORTABLE SUPPLIES OF FOODSTUFFS

Thanks to the importation of feed grains, oilcakes,
and other "raw materials" for the livestock and dairy
industries, Nazi Europe normally exports considerably
more than she imports of the various foods of animal
origin. The area is also on an export basis for one other
foodstuff important in world trade. This is the potato,
which is widely produced and consumed throughout
Europe.

A. Meat, Dairy Products, and Eggs

Important in the agricultural economy of the German
area are the meat, dairy, and egg industries—industries
that in considerable measure are dependent on imported
grains, oilcakes, and other foreign feedstuffs. Particu-

larly in the case of the principal exporting countries—
Denmark and the Netherlands—the animal population
is far in excess of what could be maintained on domestic grain and forage. Both of these countries import
feed in order to export their higher priced meats, butter,
cheese, and eggs. Elsewhere in the area these industries
are more closely geared to national resources and consumption requirements.

*Taken as a whole, the area exports more food of animal
origin than it imports.* In fact, there is little importation
of such products into any except the industrial countries
of Europe. On the other hand, production for the area
as a whole has been large. Reported production of butter
represents a little more than one-third of the world
total; of cheese, about one-half; and of milk, about one-
third. Similar comparisons cannot be made for eggs and
meat because of the unsatisfactory character of reported
data.

The table on page 48 shows the net trade of the area
by countries. Production is also indicated where reasonably satisfactory data are available.

This table shows the outstanding importance of Denmark and the Netherlands in this section of Nazi
Europe's export trade. It also shows the large production and consumption of such foods in Germany—far
larger than for any other country in the area. Poland,
too, was an important exporter of meat and eggs. The
Balkan states, important as grain exporters, play a very
minor role in the export of meat and dairy products.

The trade in meat was made up principally of large
net exports of pork and pork products, and of smaller
offsetting net imports of beef and veal. By far the
greater part of the pork exported was in the form of
bacon and ham—of which Denmark is the world's

i. trade in 1937

Countries (By groups)	Meat Trade	Butter		Cheese Trade	Milk		Eggs in Shell Trade
		Trade	Production[b]		Trade	Production[b]	
I. Bulgaria........	− .6	—	1	− 1.4	—	...	− 17.5
Rumania	− 2.7	− .1	...	—	—	...	− 10.4
Yugoslavia......	− 11.3	− .1	...	− 1.9	—	...	− 12.3
Total.........	− 14.6	− .2	1	− 3.3	—	...	− 40.2
II. Denmark........	−218.0	−152.9	183	− 9.4	− 41.1	5,300	− 96.8
Hungary........	− 4.1	− 6.0	11	− .5	− .3	....	− 11.4
Netherlands.....	− 40.9	− 53.8	103	−62.2	−523.4	5,000	− 76.2
Poland..........	− 61.4	− 8.1	...	− .5	—	...	− 26.4
Portugal........	− .2	—	...	—	—	...	− .1
Spain (1935).....	− .2	—	...	+ 1.1	...	....	− 2.9
Total.........	−324.8	−220.8	297	−71.5	−564.8	10,300	−213.8
III. Albania	—	—	1	− .8	—	1,300	− 1.3
Greece..........	+ .1	+ .3	6	− .1	+ 4.5	272	+ 1.1
Norway.........	+ 1.6	− .2	12	− 1.5	− 6.3	1,400	− 1.3
Sweden.........	− 10.9	− 23.5	72	+ .8	+ 1.7	4,300	− 2.9
Total.........	− 9.2	− 23.5	91	− 1.6	− .1	7,272	− 4.4
IV. Germany........	+ 86.9	+ 86.8	517	+36.8	+ 22.8	25,900	+ 90.2
Austria.........	+ 3.6	− 3.5	22	− 3.9	− 13.0	2,500	+ 5.1
Belgium-Luxemburg....	+ 3.4	+ 2.2	66	+22.5	+ 25.2	2,800	− 12.3
Czechoslovakia...	+ 2.3	—	...	+ .2	—	....	+ 6.7
France..........	+ 29.8	− 2.3	208	+ 2.1	− 19.6	14,700	+ 15.4
Italy...........	+ 33.7	+ 1.6	...	−19.6	− 6.8	....	+ 8.2
Switzerland.	+ 3.4	+ 2.5	27	−16.2	− 3.8	2,700	+ 14.1
Total.........	+163.1	+ 87.3	840	+21.9	+ 4.8	48,600	+127.4
All Nazi Europe......	−185.5	−157.1	1,229	−54.5	−560.1	66,172	−131.0

[a] Trade data compiled from International Institute of Agriculture, *International Yearbook of Agricultural Statistics*, 1931–32 and 1938–39. The figures for milk include condensed and powdered milk converted to fluid milk terms (1 unit of condensed milk=2.2 units of fluid, and 1 unit of powdered milk=7.7 units of fluid). Production data compiled from League of Nations, *Statistical Year-book*, 1938–39, except the 1929 figure for Rumania, which is from the League of Nations, *The Problem of Nutrition, Vol. IV* (1936).

greatest exporter. For eggs in the shell the area was on an export basis, but net imports of some 15,500 metric tons of liquid, pickled, frozen, powdered, and dried yolks and whites supplemented the supply available for consumption in the area. Of these, about two-thirds went to Germany. Fluid milk exports were small and intra-area in character, while most of the large exports of condensed and powdered milk went to external markets.

PRODUCTS, AND EGGS, 1937, 1929[a]

production, in thousands of metric tons]

II. TRADE IN 1929

Countries (By groups)	Meat Trade	Butter		Cheese Trade	Milk		Eggs in Shell Trade
		Trade	Production[b]		Trade	Production[b]	
I. Bulgaria.........	—	—	...	− 1.2	+ .2	...	− 12.7
Rumania.........	− 6.2	− .1	...	—	+ .1	1,529	− 11.6
Yugoslavia......	− 9.4	− .3	...	− 2.0	− .1	...	− 22.3
Total.........	− 15.6	− .4	...	− 3.2	+ .2	1,529	− 46.6
II. Denmark........	−252.5	−158.4	179.0	− 6.3	− 57.7	4,880	− 49.0
Hungary.........	− 3.9	− .4	4.1	− .1	+ 3.1	280	− 6.9
Netherlands.....	− 80.6	− 45.3	86.7	−95.1	−501.9	4,220	− 78.3
Poland..........	− 29.7	− 15.0	...	− 1.2	− .6	8,410	− 53.3
Portugal........	− .1	—	...	+ .4	—	...	− 8.9
Spain...........	+ 1.6	+ .1	7.6	+ 3.2	+ 1.4	1,690	+ 30.2
Total.........	−365.2	−219.0	277.4	−99.1	−555.7	19,480	−166.2
III. Albania.........	—	—	...	− 1.4	—	...	− 1.2
Greece..........	+ .3	+ .7	...	+ 1.4	+ 7.9	...	+ 2.8
Norway.........	+ 7.2	+ .1	3.8	− .2	− 26.3	1,220	− .6
Sweden.........	− 18.6	− 24.9	48.2	+ .5	+ 1.8	1,930	− 5.0
Total.........	− 11.1	− 24.1	52.0	+ .3	− 16.6	3,150	− 4.0
IV. Germany........	+ 98.9	+135.3	310.0	+64.3	+ 30.4	21,790	+167.9
Austria.........	+ 30.5	− .5	...	+ 1.2	− 2.0	...	+ 13.0
Belgium-Luxemburg....	+ 38.1	+ 2.9	62.1	+20.7	+ .2	2,830	− 43.3
Czechoslovakia...	+ 5.0	+ .1	65.0	− 1.7	− 3.0	...	+ 3.5
France..........	+ 33.6	− 3.2	219.6	+ 4.8	− 6.3	13,840	− 11.2
Italy............	+ 62.0	+ .2	42.1	−26.3	− 4.3	...	+ 6.0
Switzerland......	+ 2.5	+ 7.5	15.7	−30.6	− 75.6	2,610	+ 12.2
Total.........	+270.6	+142.3	714.5	+32.4	− 60.6	41,070	+148.1
All Nazi Europe......	−121.3	−101.2	1,043.9	−69.6	−632.7	65,229	− 68.7

[b] Production totals are incomplete, since data not available (...) are added in as if they were zeros. Also butter production shown for some countries includes creamery butter only. Coverage for milk production varies from cow's milk alone, in some cases, to milk from cows, buffaloes, goats, and ewes, in others.

The trade in meat, butter, cheese, milk, and eggs was carried on principally with countries outside the area. By far the greater part of Denmark's large exports of butter and eggs, a large percentage of the milk, and all of the bacon, went to the United Kingdom. All of the bacon exported from the Netherlands and Poland, and almost half of the Dutch milk shipped to outside markets, also went to the United Kingdom. Germany, however, was an important taker of Dutch butter, cheese, eggs, and pork products other than bacon and ham, and of the live cattle and pigs shipped from Denmark (which are not included with meat data).[13] Poland found her principal market in Austria.

The table below shows in a summary way where the area's principal producers marketed their meat and dairy products.

Where Nazi Europe's Meat and Dairy Products Were Sold, 1937[a]
(Figures in thousands of metric tons)

Market	Butter	Cheese	Milk	Bacon	Other Meat
Germany................	66	28	16	—	40
Other inside markets.....	6	42	115	—	57
United Kingdom.........	172	17	223	225	20
United States...........	1	21	10	—	20
Other outside markets....	6	17	238	—	4
Total................	251	125	602	225	141
Imports from all sources into:					
United Kingdom.....	478	149	312	352	1,095
United States.......	4	27	12	b	76

[a] Total imports of these commodities into the United Kingdom and United States are from International Institute of Agriculture, *International Yearbook of Agricultural Statistics*, 1938–39. All other data are from the official trade reports of the exporting countries, as follows:

Butter—Denmark, Netherlands, Sweden, Poland, Hungary, Austria, France.

Cheese—Netherlands, Italy, Switzerland, France, Denmark.

Milk (including fluid, condensed, and powdered)—Netherlands, Denmark, France, Switzerland.

Bacon, and other (butcher's) meat—Denmark, Netherlands, Poland, Sweden, and Yugoslavia.

[b] Included with "other meat."

The table shows the outstanding importance of the British market for German-area exporters of butter, milk, and bacon. It also indicates Britain's dependence

[13] Excluded because of the lack of conversion factors.

on these cross-channel countries—from which, in 1937, she bought 36 per cent of the butter she imported, 71 per cent of the milk, and 64 per cent of the bacon. For cheese and butcher's meat other than bacon, the trade between Britain and the area was of considerably less importance.

The area's net trade in foods of animal origin is practically the same, whether Mediterranean Asia and Africa are in or out of the reckoning. The net trade in these foods is small for each of these countries alone and for all of them combined. This is shown in detail by the table below.

TRADE OF THE MEDITERRANEAN AREA, IN MEAT AND DAIRY PRODUCTS[a]
[Net imports (+), net exports (−), in thousands of metric tons]

Territory	1937				1929			
	Meat	Butter	Cheese	Milk[b]	Meat	Butter	Cheese	Milk[b]
Mediterranean Africa:								
Algeria	− .1	+ 1.7	+ 4.8	+ 11.0	+ 2.9	+ 1.1	+ 3.7	+ 4.0
French Morocco	− 1.1	+ 1.2	+ 1.6	+ 4.0	+ 2.6	+ .4	+ 1.2	+ 2.5
Tunisia	− .4	+ .7	+ 1.2	+ 3.7	+ .8	+ .3	+ .8	+ 2.7
Egypt	+ 1.6	+ 1.0	+ 3.3	+ 2.5	+ 1.6	+ 1.0	+ 2.9	+ 1.1
Libya	—	+ .1	+ .5	+ 2.0[c]	+ .1	− .1	+ .2	+ 1.1
Spanish Morocco	+ .5	—	+ .1	+ 1.0	...	...	...	...
Tangier Zone	+ .1	+ .1	+ .1	+ .4	+ .1	—	—	+ .2
Mediterranean Asia:								
Turkey		—	+ .1	—	− .1	—	− .3	+ .4
Syria and Lebanon	+ .6	− .1	+ .1	+ .4	+ .4	− .8	+ .2	+ .7
Palestine	+ .5	+ 2.4	+ 1.1	+ 9.5	+ .2	+ .2	+ .2	+ .5
Cyprus	—	+ .1	− .1	+ .4	—	+ .1	− .3	+ 2.2
Total Mediterranean	+ 1.7	+ 7.2	+12.8	+ 34.9	+ 8.6	+ 2.2	+ 8.6	+ 15.4
Nazi Europe	−185.5	−157.1	−54.5	−560.1	−121.3	−101.2	−69.6	−632.7
Total	−183.8	−149.9	−41.7	−525.2	−112.7	− 99.0	−61.0	−617.3

[a] Compiled from sources listed in footnote *a*, table on p. 48.
[b] Including condensed and powdered in terms of fluid milk.
[c] Figure for 1936.

It seems clear that (apart from wartime destruction of the herds), so long as Europe can feed her livestock, she can consume meat and dairy products at the 1929 and 1937 levels, and also export considerable amounts to outside markets.

B. Potatoes

The potato is grown in all 20 states of the German area, yielding a crop that is considerably larger, in tonnage terms, than all of the area's cereal crops combined. And since it furnishes a plentiful crop in a land where many things are scarce, it is made to serve a wider range of purposes in Europe than in the United States. While it provides foods of various kinds for the human population, it is also used in large quantities as feed for animals and raw material for a number of industries—the most important being the distillation of alcohol that is used principally as motor fuel. In addition, it is an item of some moment in the trade of the area.

Taken as a whole, the area under German domination is a net exporter of potatoes. It is also the world's largest source of supply. In 1937 aggregate production in the area amounted to almost 154 million tons out of a world total (excluding Soviet Russia) of 186 millions. With Russia included, the world total was probably about 260 million tons, of which roughly 60 per cent were produced in Nazi Europe. The area's net exports to outside countries amounted to 483,000 tons. The net trade and production of the several states are shown in the table on page 53.

By far the largest exporter in the area—in fact, the largest in the world—is the Netherlands. Germany, the world's largest producer, imports additional quantities for domestic consumption, while Poland, the world's second largest producer, exports only a very small proportion of her crop. The Balkan states, with the exception of Hungary, have consumed practically all they produced. France, like Germany, has been on an import basis.

POTATO TRADE AND PRODUCTION 1937, 1929[a]
[In thousands of metric tons, net imports (+), net exports (−)]

Countries (By groups)	1937[b]		1929	
	Net Trade	Pro- duction	Net Trade	Pro- duction
I. Bulgaria..........	− 1	146	—	44
Rumania..........	—	2,107	− 1	2,484
Yugoslavia.......	—	1,620	+ 25	1,632
Total..........	− 1	3,873	+ 24	4,160
II. Denmark..........	− 59	1,324	+ 7	1,072
Hungary..........	− 79	2,559	− 61	2,224
Netherlands.......	−459	2,651	−563	4,097
Poland...........	− 47	40,221	− 77	31,750
Portugal..........	− 4	596	+ 62	345
Spain.............	− 67	5,064	− 46	4,623
Total..........	−715	52,415	−678	44,111
III. Albania..........	—	3	—	—
Greece...........	+ 3	193	+ 32	35
Norway..........	− 1	861	− 1	900
Sweden..........	+ 6	1,887	+ 1	1,885
Total..........	+ 8	2,944	+ 32	2,820
IV. Germany..........	+121	55,310	+195	40,077
Austria...........	+ 21	3,612	+ 39	2,803
Belgium-Luxemburg	+ 4	3,091	− 76	4,148
Czechoslovakia.....	− 1	12,363	− 19	10,696
France...........	+106	15,878	+191	16,175
Italy.............	− 78	3,214	− 39	2,008
Switzerland.......	+ 52	878	+ 56	778
Total..........	+225	94,346	+347	76,685
All Nazi Europe........	−483	153,578	−275	127,776
WORLD PRODUCTION.....	186,000[c]		202,620	

[a] Compiled from International Institute of Agriculture, *International Year-book of Agricultural Statistics*, 1931–32 and 1938–39.
[b] Figures for Spain are for 1935, the latest available.
[c] Excluding U.S.S.R. In 1935 Russia produced 69.7 million metric tons.

More than half of the potato trade has been intra-area in character. Of the 945,000 metric tons shipped out in

1937 by the principal exporting countries of the area, 537,000 found a market in countries inside the area:[14]

Markets Inside the Area	Thousands of Metric Tons
Germany........................	150
Belgium-Luxemburg.............	94
France.........................	84
Italy...........................	67
Other internal markets...........	142
Total.........................	537

The outside markets for potatoes have been widely distributed. Argentina was by far the largest taker in 1937. The United Kingdom—which in 1929 outranked all other outside markets—in 1937 took less than half the quantity shipped to Argentina. North Africa and the Far East also imported potatoes from Europe in appreciable amounts. The figures below (in thousands of metric tons) show the principal outlets for the potatoes shipped outside the area, and the total potato imports of these countries.

Outside Markets	Imports from Nazi Europe	Total Imports
Argentina.......................	173	242
United Kingdom................	81	226
French North Africa[15]..........	56	61
Egypt.........................	19	22
British India and Ceylon........	15	...
Uruguay.......................	14	33
Other outside markets...........	50	...
Total.........................	408	

---

[14] The 7 principal exporting countries were the Netherlands, Denmark, Poland, Italy, France, Hungary, and Belgium-Luxemburg, their exports accounting for 945,000 of the total 1,086,000 for the whole area. Figures

Potato imports into Mediterranean Asia and Africa partly offset the net exports from Nazi Europe. The amounts involved for the individual Mediterranean countries are not large, but in the aggregate they would represent a reduction of some 15 or 16 per cent in the export surplus of the European area—according to the figures for 1929 and 1937. This is shown by the figures below, which give net trade in thousands of metric tons.[16]

	1937		1929	
Nazi Europe	−483		−275	
Mediterranean Africa:				
Algeria	+34		− 1	
French Morocco	+ 4		+11	
Tunisia	+10		+13	
Egypt	+19		+21	
Libya	+ 4		+ 2	
Spanish Morocco	+ 3		...	
Tangier Zone	+ 4	+ 78	+ 3	+ 49
Mediterranean Asia:				
Turkey	—		+ 4	
Syria and Lebanon	− 6		+ 2	
Palestine	+18		+ 7	
Cyprus	−17	− 5	−16	− 3
Total	−410		−229	

It seems reasonably clear that an exportable supply of potatoes can easily be produced in the area. But judging from the experience of recent years, this export balance will be larger if the area does not extend into the Mediterranean territories.

---

showing distribution of the exports of these countries were compiled from their official trade reports.

[15] Including French Morocco and Tangier, Algeria, Tunisia.

[16] Net imports (+), net exports (−). Compiled from sources listed in footnote *a* to table on p. 53.

SUMMARY

The trade figures given above for the principal food-stuffs moving in world trade indicate that, on the whole, the shortages for the larger area now under German domination are even larger than those for the old Reich. In only a few cases has the expansion over additional territory brought a shift from an import to an export basis, while for most commodities, net imports for the larger area are two or more times as great as for Germany alone. This is shown in summary form by the accompanying chart.

Net Trade in Principal Foodstuffs, 1937
Germany and Nazi Europe Compared

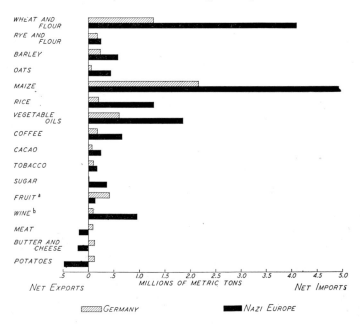

a Includes raisins, grapes, citrus fruits, and bananas.
b The unit for wine is 10,000 hectoliters.

In some commodities, the larger area is more nearly self-sufficing—that is, it produces a larger proportion of its food requirements—than the old Reich; in others there has been a shift in the opposite direction. On the whole, imports have accounted for 9 to 10 per cent of the cereals consumed in Nazi Europe; for about half of the vegetable oils—and for the greater part of the oil-cakes used in the dairy industry; for all of the coffee, tea, and cacao, and for roughly one-third of the tobacco consumption. In sugar, fruit, and wine, production has almost equalled consumption. In meat, dairy products, eggs, and potatoes, the area has been on an export basis.

Western Hemisphere countries supplied more than 60 per cent of Europe's grain, roughly 15 per cent of the vegetable oils, the greater part of the coffee, and about half of the tobacco imported into Nazi Europe. The rest of the vegetable oil and tobacco imports were accounted for by the Far East and tropical Africa. Cacao came principally from tropical Africa, wine from Algeria, and tea from the Far East. The United Kingdom offered by far the best market for the area's exports of meat, dairy products, and eggs, while potatoes went to Argentina, the United Kingdom, and French North Africa.

CHAPTER III

SHORTAGES OF AGRICULTURAL AND FORESTRY RAW MATERIALS

Among the agricultural and forestry products that serve as raw materials for industry, a few commodities are of outstanding importance: the textile fibers, rubber, cattle hides, and timber and woodpulp. Available supplies of these materials, and of the industrial minerals considered in Chapter IV, constitute one of the limiting factors determining Nazi Europe's output of manufactures for domestic consumption and for export. For all of them, with the single exception of woodpulp, the area has been on an import basis.

I. COTTON

In value terms—though not in volume—cotton has long been the world's leading agricultural export. By the same token, its value in international trade exceeds that of any other textile fiber. In recent years, progress made in perfecting the use of substitute materials has undoubtedly tended to restrict its consumption, in spite of the price reduction that has accompanied the depression. However, the volume moving in world trade was only 4 per cent lower in 1937 than in 1929.

Nazi Europe imports practically all of the cotton consumed by its industries. In 1929, the cotton production of the area was only 6,000 metric tons, compared with net imports of 1,437,000 tons. For 1937, production was 35,000 and net imports 1,350,000 tons. Trade and production data by countries—grouped, as in preceding chapters, according to the character of their trade—are given in the accompanying table.

Cotton Trade and Production, 1937, 1929[a]
(In thousands of metric tons)

Countries (By groups)	1937[b]		1929	
	Net Imports	Produc-tion	Net Imports	Produc-tion
I. Bulgaria..............	10	10	2	1
Rumania..............	17	1	3	—
Yugoslavia...........	21	1	8	—
Total..............	48	12	13	1
II. Denmark.............	9	—	5	—
Hungary.............	24	—	12	—
Netherlands..........	62	—	47	—
Poland..............	72	—	61	—
Portugal.............	30	—	16	—
Spain...............	99	3	76	1
Total..............	296	3	217	1
III. Albania..............	—	—	—	—
Greece..............	3	16	3	3
Norway.............	4	—	2	—
Sweden.............	34	—	22	—
Total..............	41	16	27	3
IV. Germany.............	245	—	315	—
Austria..............	39	—	29	—
Belgium-Luxemburg....	97	—	86	—
Czechoslovakia........	105	—	119	—
France..............	279	—	357	—
Italy...............	166	4	244	1
Switzerland...........	34	—	30	—
Total..............	965	4	1,180	1
All Nazi Europe...........	1,350	35	1,437	6

[a] Compiled from International Institute of Agriculture, *International Yearbook of Agricultural Statistics*, 1931–32, and 1938–39.
[b] Figures for Spain are for 1935, the latest available.

Taken as a whole, the 20 states of the area consumed 25 per cent of world production in 1929; and 17 per cent of the larger crop grown in 1937. All of them are cotton importers (although the amounts taken by Albania are of negligible proportions). None of them rank among the important producers of the world. The area's largest consumer has been the textile industry of France, with German mills taking some 10 per cent less than the French.

The United States is and long has been the principal source of cotton for Nazi Europe. India has stood second to the United States, both as a producer and as an exporter to the European market, in the two years considered here. These, and other sources of supply, are listed in the accompanying table, which shows their exports to Nazi Europe, and also their total exports and production in 1937 and 1929.

OUTSIDE SOURCES SUPPLYING COTTON, 1937, 1929[a]
(Figures in thousands of metric tons)

Exporting Country	1937			1929		
	Exports to Nazi Europe	Total Exports	Production	Exports to Nazi Europe	Total Exports	Production
Western Hemisphere:						
United States.......	633	1,377	4,108	977	1,809	3,214
Brazil..............	124	236	450	3	49	127
Peru...............	29	81	82	3	45	66
Mexico.............	10	10	74	2	17	53
Four countries.....	796	1,704	4,714	985	1,920	3,460
India (including Burma) and Ceylon.........	209	673	1,076	256	715	951
Egypt...............	207	400	495	138	343	383
Belgian Congo........	47	47	38	5	10	7
Turkey..............	13	13	65	6	16	22
Total for sources listed..	1,272	2,837	6,388	1,390	3,004	4,823
WORLD TOTAL[b].........	1,394	3,276	8,240	1,554[b]	3,407	5,756

[a] See footnote *a*, p. 59, for sources of data. Trade figures for the Belgian Congo may include some cotton grown in nearby territories.
[b] Including intra-area trade of Nazi Europe.

Some sizeable shifts in the trade are shown by the table, particularly as regards the Western Hemisphere. In 1929 the United States supplied Europe with 977,000 tons of cotton, or 63 per cent of the area's imports. But in 1937 only 633,000 tons, or 45 per cent of Europe's imports, were taken from the United States. In the meantime, other Western Hemisphere countries took over part of the market thus lost to producers in the United States. Brazil gained most from this shift, her share in the shipments to Europe amounting to a negligible fraction of 1 per cent in 1929, compared with 9 per cent in 1937.

European demand for cotton is a matter of great importance to the principal producing countries. In the United States, where more than half of the world's crop is grown, shipments to Nazi Europe accounted for 30 per cent of the crop, and 54 per cent of total cotton exports, in 1929. In 1937, only 15 per cent of the crop and 46 per cent of the greatly reduced volume of cotton exports went to those markets. And as a result of this shrinkage in demand for the American products, the cotton-growing South has been forced to explore the possibilities offered by greater diversification in agriculture, and also in industry. India, the world's second largest producer and exporter of cotton, sent 27 per cent of her 1929 crop and 19 per cent of her 1937 crop to the Nazi area. Egypt marketed 42 per cent of her 1937 crop there, and Brazil 28 per cent.

With all of Mediterranean Africa and Asia inside its boundaries, the area would still import roughly two-thirds of its cotton supply. So extended, it would include only one important cotton-producing country, Egypt. To be sure, some of the other Mediterranean countries are also net exporters of cotton, but the amounts involved are extremely small. This is shown by the figures for net trade given below in thousands of metric tons—the plus sign indicating net imports, and the minus sign net exports.

	1937		1929	
Nazi Europe...............		+1,350		+1,437
Mediterranean Africa:				
Algeria...................	− .1		− 1	
French Morocco...........	—		—	
Tunisia..................	—		—	
Egypt....................	−400		−343	
Libya....................	—		—	
Spanish Morocco..........	+ .1	− 400	—	− 344
Mediterranean Asia:				
Turkey...................	− 11		− 16	
Syria and Lebanon.........	− 3		− 1	
Palestine.................	+ .7		—	
Cyprus...................	− .3	− 13.6	− 1	− 18
		+936.4		+1,075

In short, there is little likelihood that the German area will achieve self-sufficiency in cotton. In saying this, we are judging from past records, and taking into account the efforts that have been made to find substitutes and to increase the cotton crop of southern Europe and of trans-Mediterranean countries. Numerous conjectures have been offered, of course, concerning the outlook for future independence, through the use of new substitute fibers—produced from unspecified materials and sources. At the beginning of the 1940's, however, such independence from imported cotton is still unrealized.

II. WOOL

Among the textile fibers, wool is second only to cotton in the value and volume moving in world trade. And like cotton, it is the necessary raw material for a large group of industries that turn out yarn and cloth for European consumption and for export. For most uses it is a commodity that has no substitute, in spite of much chemical research spent on finding one. While imitation fibers of various kinds have offered some competition in recent years, wool production and trade have remained reasonably stable in volume terms, though wool prices have declined sharply since 1929.

In wool, as in cotton, Nazi Europe depends on outside sources for most of the raw material used in the spinning and weaving industries. All of the 20 countries produce wool, but their aggregate production is considerably below their requirements. In 1937, for example, the domestic crop of these countries was only 38 per cent as large in volume as their net imports. In 1929 it was only 30 per cent as large. The table on page 64 gives net trade and production data for both years.

In 1929 some 63,000 tons of wool, or 10 per cent of the world's crop, were produced in the area, and about 45 per cent were consumed there. Production remained at approximately the same level in 1937, but imports and consumption both declined. Rumania, Spain, and France are the principal producers. Germany, France, Belgium, and Italy are the principal importers and consumers.

British Empire sources normally provide the bulk of the wool imports. At the top of the list is Australia, supplying about 35 per cent of the total, while other British countries together supply about half as much as Australia. Three South American countries together account

WOOL TRADE AND PRODUCTION, 1937, 1929[a]
(In thousands of metric tons of washed wool[b])

Countries (By groups)	1937[c]		1929	
	Net Imports (+) Net Exports (−)	Production	Net Imports (+) Net Exports (−)	Production
I. Bulgaria............	+ .6	3.3	+ .9	3.4
Rumania............	+ .6	10.4	+ 1.2	8.5
Yugoslavia.........	+ 2.3	5.2	+ 2.0	4.3
Total............	+ 3.5	18.9	+ 4.1	16.2
II. Denmark...........	+ 2.0	.2	+ 1.6	.2
Hungary...........	+ .1	2.4	− 1.4	2.2
Netherlands........	+ 2.6	.4	+ 2.6	.4
Poland.............	+ 8.9	1.9	+ 8.5	1.6
Portugal...........	− .8	3.2	− .6	3.2
Spain..............	+ 1.6	10.5	− .8	13.2
Total............	+ 14.4	18.6	+ 9.9	20.8
III. Albania............	− 1.3	.8	− .6	.6
Greece.............	+ 1.9	2.9	+ .9	1.6
Norway............	+ .9	.9	—	.8
Sweden............	+ 8.9	.2	+ 7.5	.3
Total............	+ 10.4	4.8	+ 7.8	3.3
IV. Germany...........	+ 46.3	6.9	+ 60.2	5.1
Austria............	+ 4.5	.2	+ 4.2	.2
Belgium-Luxemburg	+ 16.9	.1	+ 14.6	.1
Czechoslovakia.....	+ 8.0	.4	+ 8.2	.4
France.............	+ 40.9	8.8	+ 76.8	9.1
Italy..............	+ 16.3	4.8	+ 20.5	7.9
Switzerland........	+ 5.9	.1	+ 8.1	.1
Total............	+138.8	21.3	+192.6	22.9
All Nazi Europe........	+167.1	63.6	+214.4	63.2

[a] Trade data were compiled from International Institute of Agriculture, *International Yearbook of Agricultural Statistics*, 1931–32, and 1938–39; production data from League of Nations, *Statistical Year-book*, 1938–39.

[b] Where necessary, conversion has been made from greasy wool to washed wool. The experts estimate that washed wool weighs about 30 to 40 per cent as much as greasy, and assume a general average of 35 per cent.

[c] Production and trade for Spain and production for Rumania are for 1935, the latest data available.

for 17 per cent or more of the total. The principal sources of supply are shown in the accompanying table.

PRINCIPAL OUTSIDE SOURCES FOR WOOL, 1937, 1929[a]
(In thousands of metric tons of washed wool[b])

Exporting Country	1937			1929		
	Exports to Nazi Europe	Total Exports	Production	Exports to Nazi Europe	Total Exports	Production
British Empire:						
Australia............	80.2	140.2	160.3	91.3	134.7	148.9
New Zealand........	10.5	59.0	47.1	3.1	48.1	41.5
Union of South Africa	22.3	39.9	40.5	31.2	47.6	52.7
United Kingdom[c]....	14.1	15.6	17.0	24.4	84.8	17.8
India..............	1.9	21.1	15.8	1.7	15.2	15.8
South America:						
Argentina..........	25.7	53.1	60.3	39.9	50.9	56.0
Uruguay...........	7.5	17.1	17.0	9.3	19.4	28.7
Chile..............	3.7	4.3	5.7	2.4	4.0	4.7
French North Africa...	6.4	10.8	12.3	5.3	5.4	10.0
Total for sources listed..	172.3	361.1	376.0	208.6	410.1	376.1
WORLD TOTAL.........	214.6[d]	...	626.0	263.7[d]	...	631.0

[a] Exports to Nazi Europe for 1937 are from League of Nations, *International Trade in Certain Raw Materials and Foodstuffs*, 1938; for 1929 from official trade statistics of importing countries. Total exports are from International Institute of Agriculture, *International Yearbook of Agricultural Statistics*, 1931–32 and 1938–39; and production figures are from League of Nations, *Statistical Year-book*, 1938–39.
[b] See footnote *b* to table, p. 64.
[c] The United Kingdom is a large net importer of wool, but also a re-exporter.
[d] This figure represents total imports of Nazi Europe, as contrasted with the net import total shown on p. 64.

A glance at the table shows the high degree of inter-dependence existing between the wool manufacturers of Europe and this important group of wool growers. Around 75 to 80 per cent of the area's wool imports come from these 8 producing countries. And vice versa, roughly 50 per cent of their wool crop normally has gone to the European market.

Mediterranean Asia and Africa export wool, but their net exports are small in comparison with the import requirements of Nazi Europe. By combining the trade of these two areas, the net imports shown for 1929 are reduced from 214,000 to 188,000 metric tons and for 1937, from 167,000 to 144,000. The net trade for the two areas is shown by the figures below, in thousands of metric tons of washed wool—the plus sign indicating net imports and the minus sign net exports.[1]

	1937		1929	
Nazi Europe..............	+167.1		+214.4	
Mediterranean Africa:				
Algeria...................	− 2.4		− 1.0	
French Morocco...........	− 5.4		− 2.0	
Tunisia..................	− .7		—	
Egypt....................	− .9		− .8	
Libya....................	− 1.2		− .5	
Spanish Morocco.........	—		—	
Tangier..................	—	− 10.6	—	− 4.3
Mediterranean Asia:				
Turkey...................	−11.0		−16.0	
Syria and Lebanon.........	− 1.3		− 5.5	
Palestine................	− .2		− .3	
Cyprus..................	− .4	− 12.9	− .3	− 22.1
Total..................		+143.6		+188.0

Consumption, as shown by the trade and production figures for this larger area, amounted to roughly 235,000 metric tons of washed wool in 1937, and 271,000 in 1929. And, therefore—if changes in the storage supply

[1] Sources are listed in footnote *a*, table on p. 64.

are left out of account—the figures indicate that more than 60 per cent of the raw wool used in the industry of this larger area has been provided by net imports from outside sources.

III. OTHER TEXTILE RAW MATERIALS

Silk, flax, hemp, and jute are the other natural fibers that have long been used in the textile industry. In addition, fibers of synthetic origin are being produced—from woodpulp, from coal and air, from milk, and from other substances—with a view to reducing imports of some one or more of the natural fibers. These new materials have been particularly effective as substitutes for silk and are gradually reducing its importance in world industry and trade.

Nazi Europe is a net importer of raw silk, but in decreasing quantities. Production in the area has also diminished during the past decade. Net imports of raw silk stood at 3,230 metric tons in 1929, reduced to 2,360 in 1937; and production during the same period was reduced from 5,680 to 3,700. Trade and production data for these years are given in the table on page 68.

The only producer of any moment was Italy, whose output in 1937 made up 86 per cent of the total for the area, but less than 6 per cent of the world total. The principal importer was France, a country long famous for silk manufactures.

The area's total silk imports in 1937 amounted to 4,970 metric tons, half of which came from the world's principal producer, Japan. The rest was accounted for principally by imports from China and by intra-area shipments—from Italy into Germany, France, and other parts of the area. The importance of the European

RAW SILK TRADE AND PRODUCTION, BY COUNTRIES, 1937, 1929[a]

[In thousands of metric tons; net imports (+), net exports (−)]

Countries (By groups)	1937		1929	
	Net Trade[b]	Pro-duction	Net Trade	Pro-duction
I. Bulgaria.............	+ .02	.14	− .18	.20
Rumania............	—	.02	+ .02	.04
Yugoslavia.........	− .01	.04	− .08	.11
Total.............	+ .01	.20	− .24	.35
II. Denmark............	+ .12	—	—	—
Hungary............	− .01	.02	+ .05	.05
Poland.............	+ .04	—	+ .06	—
Spain..............	+ .03	.02	+ .22	.07
Total.............	+ .18	.04	+ .33	.12
III. Greece..............	—	.24	− .11	.18
IV. Germany............	+1.26	—	+2.36	—
Austria.............	+ .02	—	− .01	—
France.............	+2.46	.05	+5.26	.20
Italy..............	−1.82	3.17	−4.83	4.83
Switzerland.........	+ .25	—	+ .47	—
Total.............	+2.17	3.22	+3.25	5.03
All Nazi Europe.........	+2.36	3.70	+3.23	5.68

[a] Net trade compiled from International Institute of Agriculture, *International Yearbook of Agricultural Statistics*, 1931–32 and 1938–39; production from League of Nations, *Statistical Year-book*, 1938–39. For the seven countries in the area which are omitted from this table, silk trade and production were negligible.

[b] Net trade for Spain is for 1935, the latest figure available.

market to leading silk producers in 1937 is indicated by the comparisons given below for 1937—in thousands of metric tons of raw silk.[2]

[2] World exports, as given by the International Institute of Agriculture (*International Yearbook of Agricultural Statistics*, 1938–39), amounted to 38,540 metric tons. Incomplete totals of 54,100 for world production in 1937, and of 60,770 in 1929 were reported by the League of Nations (*Statistical Yearbook*, 1938–39), China being one of the countries for which complete

Exporting Country	Exports to Nazi Europe	Total Exports	Production
Japan......................	2.39	28.47	41.87
China......................	.86	4.11	4.91
Other outside sources..........	.71	3.23	3.44
Italy.......................	1.01	2.07	3.17

Only 8 per cent of Japan's total exports of raw silk went to Europe in 1937—and only 6 per cent of her total production. Imports from other producing areas were smaller in absolute amounts, but were more important in comparison with the total.

The German area imports part of the flax and hemp and all of the jute consumed by its industries. This group of countries produces roughly 21 per cent of the world's flax crop and 33 per cent of the hemp. In addition they import some 10 to 20 per cent of the flax they consume and about 15 per cent of the hemp. Jute, however, is a product peculiar to Asia, with India alone accounting for more than 99 per cent of world production. The table on page 70 shows the area's production of two of these fibers, and net trade in all three of them.

Poland has long been the principal flax producer of the area. Flax imports, with little if any exception, have come from Soviet states, which produce roughly 77 per cent of the world's supply. Looked at from the Russian point of view, about 18 per cent of the flax exported by the Soviet states, but only 3 per cent of their production, finds a market in the German-controlled area.

Italy is the principal hemp producer and exporter of Nazi Europe. In fact, the type of hemp grown

---

data are not available. It is probable that a small part of the 710 tons of exports to Nazi Europe attributed to "other outside sources" may have come from small producers inside the area.

throughout the area—and also in the Russian-controlled states and Ireland—goes by the name of Italian hemp, and is somewhat different from the "Manila hemp" of the Philippines—though both answer the same purposes. The hemp imports of the area come principally from the Soviet states, the Philippines, and China.

CURRENT SUPPLIES OF FLAX, HEMP, AND JUTE, 1937, 1929ᵃ

[In thousands of metric tons, net imports (+), net exports (−)]

Countries (By groups)	1937ᵇ Flax Net Trade	Flax Production	Hemp Net Trade	Hemp Production	Jute (Net Trade)	1929 Flax Net Trade	Flax Production	Hemp Net Trade	Hemp Production	Jute (Net trade)
I. Bulgaria	—	1	—	5	+ 1	+ 1	c		1	—
Rumania	d	9	+ 2	27	+ 5	—	3	+ 1	19	—
Yugoslavia		11	−17	50	+ 4	d	9	−11	26	—
Total	—	21	−15	82	+ 10	+ 1	12	−10	46	—
II. Denmark	+ 1	—	+ 3	—	+ 1	—	—	+ 3	—	—
Hungary	− 4	3	− 2	13	+ 15	− 5	4	—	7	+ 11
Netherlands	−11	15	+ 4	—	+ 16	− 9	15	+10	—	+ 13
Poland	−18	38	—	12	+ 13	−16	66	− 1	22	+ 27
Portugal	+ 1	—	c		+ 5	+ 1	—	—	—	—
Spain	+ 2	—	c	5	+ 55	+ 1	—	+ 1	7	+ 51
Total	−29	56	+ 5	30	+105	−28	85	+13	36	+102
III. Albania	—	—	—	—	—	—	—	—	—	—
Greece	—	—	+ 2	—	+ 3	—	—	+ 2	—	+ 1
Norway	—	—	+ 4	—	+ 1	—	—	+ 3	—	+ 1
Sweden	+ 3	—	+ 9	—	+ 8	+ 2	—	+ 7	—	+ 61
Total	+ 3	—	+15	—	+ 12	+ 2	—	+12	—	+ 63
IV. Germany	+13	34	+48	7	+109	+10	11ᵉ	+27	—	+141
Austria	+ 1	1	+ 7	—	+ 8	+ 1	1	+ 7	—	+ 12
Belgium-Luxemburg	−14	24	+ 7	—	+ 64	−12	19	+11	—	+ 32
Czecho-slovakia	+17	11	+ 4	5	+ 42	+22	9	+ 5	6	+ 36
France	+21	19	+19	4	+ 98	+40	39	+32	5	+118
Italy	—	3	−47	109	+ 43	+ 1	3	−64	90	+ 59
Switzerland	+ 6	—	c	—	+ 1	+ 4	—	c	—	—
Total	+44	92	+38	125	+365	+66	82	+18	101	+398
All Nazi Europe	+18	169	+43	237	+492	+41	179	+33	183	+563

ᵃ Compiled from International Institute of Agriculture, *International Yearbook of Agricultural Statistics*, 1931–32, and 1938–39. Flax tow and hemp tow are included in most cases in both trade and production. Net trade in hemp includes imports of manila hemp. Trade in raw flax, which was reported for Netherlands, Belgium, and France, has been converted to fiber and tow on the basis of 100 tons of raw=5.9 tons of fiber and 1.4 tons of tow and pluckings (see *Encyclopaedia Britannica*, 14th ed., under "Flax").
ᵇ Figures for Spain are for 1935, the latest available.
ᶜ Included with flax.
ᵈ Included with hemp.
ᵉ Estimated from 1929 area in production and from average yield per hectare in 1931.

Jute imports, of necessity, are from India. They represent about 60 per cent of the jute export trade from India, and about 33 per cent of the Indian crop.

The countries of Mediterranean Africa and Asia produce and consume very little, if any, raw silk, flax, hemp, or jute. Extension of Nazi control across the Mediterranean, therefore, would make no change in the import requirements for these fibers.

IV. RUBBER

Rubber is one of the commodities for which synthetic substitutes are available—at a price. Nazi Germany, the first to produce this new *ersatz* in commercial quantities, manufactured enough in 1937 to supply 5 per cent of her consumptive requirements, increased to 22 per cent in 1938 when operations were begun in a number of large plants. The future supply to be afforded by this new industry should not be overlooked, therefore, in any discussion of the natural rubber supply, although it was of little importance in 1937, and none at all in 1929.

In rubber the area is decidedly vulnerable. Prior to 1938, practically all of the rubber consumed in Nazi Europe came from outside sources of supply. Synthetic rubber, as indicated above, was meeting only a small fraction of Germany's needs, and the developed plant capacity of that country was, of course, far from sufficient to provide exports to neighboring states. Germany, France, and Italy were the large consumers of natural rubber, their net imports amounting to more than 70 per cent of the total for the area. Net imports of the 20 states are shown on page 72, in thousands of metric tons.[3]

[3] Compiled from International Institute of Agriculture, *International Yearbook of Agricultural Statistics*, 1931–32 and 1938–39. Net imports for Spain are for 1935. The 1929 figures indicate that Switzerland was exporting from storage.

Country	1937	1929	Country	1937	1929
I. Bulgaria	.7	—	III. Albania	—	—
Rumania	1.8	.4	Greece	.1	—
Yugoslavia	3.0	.3	Norway	2.1	3.3
			Sweden	6.8	3.8
Total	5.5	.7			
			Total	9.0	7.1
II. Denmark	2.2	.8	IV. Germany	99.7	49.9
Hungary	3.5	1.3	Austria	3.8	3.5
Netherlands	4.4	5.0	Belgium-Luxemburg	15.2	9.8
Poland	6.2	4.0	Czechoslovakia	13.3	4.8
Portugal	.8	—	France	66.7	68.5
Spain	8.7	2.2	Italy	25.4	17.0
			Switzerland	1.0	−.6
Total	25.8	13.3			
			Total	225.1	152.9
			Total, Nazi Europe	265.4	174.0

Nazi Europe's principal sources of rubber are certain Far Eastern members of the British and Dutch Empires. In 1929 one-third of the area's supply was imported from British India, but by 1937 first place had shifted to British Malaya, which furnished 57 per cent of the total. In both years the Dutch East Indies were the second largest source of area imports.

The table on page 73 shows the amounts imported from the principal rubber-producing countries of the world, and the significance of the area as a market for their product.

As the table shows, Nazi area imports in recent years have accounted for 20 per cent or more of the world exports of rubber.[4] In the case of British Malaya, where

[4] Compared with 40 per cent to the United States and 10 per cent to Britain.

rubber is the principal export, shipments to the German area represented 12 per cent of the value of total exports of all commodities. For the Dutch East Indies, whose production is more varied in character, such shipments accounted for 3 per cent of total exports. For other producers this trade was of relatively little importance.

PRINCIPAL OUTSIDE SOURCE FOR RUBBER, 1937, 1929[a]
(In thousands of metric tons)

Exporting Country	1937		1929	
	Exports to Nazi Europe	Total[b] Exports	Exports to Nazi Europe	Total[b] Exports
British Malaya...............	150	693	13	422
Dutch East Indies............	44	446	31	301
India, Burma, and Ceylon.....	21	87	60	88
French Indo-China	19	45	5	10
Brazil......................	8	15	7	20
Africa......................	7	10	4	6
Total for sources listed........	249	1,296	120	847
WORLD TOTAL[c]...............	271	1,430	188	1,178

[a] Exports to Nazi Europe for 1937 compiled from League of Nations' *International Trade in Certain Raw Materials and Foodstuffs*, 1938; for 1929 compiled from the official trade reports of the importing countries. Total exports and world totals compiled from International Institute of Agriculture, *International Yearbook of Agricultural Statistics*, 1931–32, and 1938–39.

[b] For rubber, total exports give a better indication of the world supply than available production figures, since the latter include plantation rubber only.

[c] The world totals given here include the re-export trade in rubber—for example, from the United States, Great Britain, and various parts of the Nazi area—most of which originally came from the sources listed above.

The Mediterranean countries of Africa and Asia produce no rubber, and import very little. In 1929 net imports of crude rubber, as shown by the trade reports of these countries, were 1,000 metric tons, and in 1937 only one-tenth of that amount.

V. HIDES AND SKINS

Raw hides and skins of all kinds made up 1.7 per cent of the aggregate value of world exports in 1937, and 1.8 per cent in 1929. Cattle hides, the most important item in the group, accounted for somewhat less than half the total in both years. The Western Hemisphere supplies about half the cattle hides moving in world trade, while continental Europe (excluding Russia) provides a market for about the same amount.

All countries of Nazi Europe, with two minor exceptions, were on an import basis for cattle hides in 1937. The figures below show the net imports and total exports of the area in thousands of metric tons.[5]

Countries (By groups)	Net Im- ports	Total Ex- ports	Countries (By groups)	Net Im- ports	Total Ex- ports
I. Bulgaria	4	—	III. Albania	−1	1
Rumania	—	—	Greece	5	—
Yugoslavia	5	—	Norway	2	4
			Sweden	4	11
Total	9	—			
			Total	10	16
II. Denmark	−4	8	IV. Germany	110	1
Hungary	8	—	Austria	2	3
Netherlands	11	31	Belgium-Luxemburg	7	18
Poland	20	1	Czechoslovakia	24	6
Portugal	4	—	France	3	31
Spain (1935)	4	1	Italy	21	4
			Switzerland	3	4
Total	43	41			
			Total	170	67
			All Nazi Europe	232	124

[5] The figures are from the League of Nations, *International Trade in Certain Raw Materials and Foodstuffs*, 1938, and include both wet and dry hides. Figures for Spain are from the same, 1936 edition. Here we have used 1935 data for Spain, although figures are available for 1937—a highly abnormal year in Spain.

Production figures are not published for cattle hides so that the share of consumption supplied from domestic sources cannot be measured here. The largest importer was Germany, whose net imports amounted to 110,000 metric tons, out of 232,000 for the whole area. France, Belgium, and the Netherlands were all active as middlemen in the intra-area trade of the 20 countries. Denmark and Albania were the only states reporting any net exports.

The greater part of the imported hides came from South American countries. A much smaller proportion was shipped from British Empire markets. The table below shows the source of imports in more detail, and indicates the importance of European purchases in the cattle hides trade. The figures are for 1937—in thousands of metric tons.

Exporting Country	Exports to Nazi Europe	Total Exports
South America:		
Argentina..................	75	142
Brazil....................	41	63
Uruguay..................	15	22
Colombia.................	7	8
Mexico.....................	7	7
British Empire:		
India.....................	15	26
South Africa..............	10	12
United Kingdom[6]..........	8	8
Australia.................	4	17
Madagascar.................	6	8
French North Africa.........	2	9

[6] The United Kingdom is a net importer of cattle hides.

About one-half the cattle hides shipped from the world's principal producer, Argentina, were sold to the countries of continental Europe. For most of the other producing countries, this market was of even greater importance, taking two-thirds of the shipments from Brazil and Uruguay, and even larger shares from some of the others.

With the area extended to include Mediterranean Asia and Africa, Nazi Europe's import requirements for hides and skins would show little change. Small imports into some of these countries would practically offset the small exports from others, leaving a very small net figure for all of them combined.

VI. TIMBER AND WOODPULP

Shipments of timber in recent years have made up about $2\frac{1}{4}$ per cent of the value of world exports, and woodpulp an additional 1 per cent or more.[7] Meantime, world consumption of timber in the construction of buildings and bridges and the manufacture of furniture and vehicles is losing ground to other substances—iron and steel, cement and bricks, and the new plastics that the chemist is evolving from pulp made partly from wood and partly from soy beans and other farm crops. Woodpulp, on the other hand, is being used in increasing amounts in the paper and textile industries, in the manufacture of munitions, and also, as indicated above, in the manufacture of new plastics. Both timber and woodpulp are commodities in which there is an active trade in continental Europe.

Taken as a whole, the area is a net importer of timber

---

[7] Timber includes sawlogs, whether rough hewn or not, sawn wood, planed wood, pulpwood, pit-props, and railway ties. Figures are based on *Statistisches Jahrbuch fuer das Deutsche Reich*, 1938, p. 158*.

and a net exporter of woodpulp. To combine the trade figures for timber and woodpulp it is, of course, necessary to reduce them to a common unit—preferably, to reduce the woodpulp data to pulpwood equivalents. No generally acceptable conversion factor is available for this calculation, but a rough approximation, based on

TIMBER AND WOODPULP TRADE, 1937, 1929[a]
(In millions of solid cubic meters)

Kind of Wood	1937			1929		
	Nazi Europe		World Exports	Nazi Europe		World Exports
	Im- ports	Ex- ports		Im- ports	Ex- ports	
Sawn and hewn, and saw-logs:						
Softwood (conifer)....	11.9	12.2	33.3	19.8	17.2	44.4
Hardwood..........	1.9	1.4	6.4	2.6	1.6	5.3
Pit-props and railway ties.	1.7	2.5	7.9	2.5	4.3	8.7
Pulpwood..............	5.8	1.5	9.8	6.2	2.9	10.4
Total timber..........	21.3	17.6	57.4	31.1	26.0	68.8
Woodpulp in terms of wood (rough approximation)[b].	7.8	16.1	27.8	6.5	12.2	18.7
Woodpulp—in millions of metric tons of pulp......	*1.8*	*3.7*	*6.4*	*1.5*	*2.8*	*4.3*

[a] Data for 1937 compiled principally from League of Nations, *International Trade in Certain Raw Materials and Foodstuffs*, 1938, and from Comité Internationale du Bois, *Year-Book of World Timber Trade*, 1938; 1929 principally from *Statistisches Jahrbuch fuer das Deutsche Reich*, and from official trade reports. Woodpulp imports for 1929 are overstated—see note *a* to table on p. 79.

[b] The experts point out that the ratio of woodpulp to pulpwood varies for different woods and different processes of manufacture. However, a rough measure is all that is required here. The ratio used (1 metric ton of woodpulp = 4.34 solid cubic meters of pulpwood) is computed from data for pulpwood consumption and woodpulp production in the United States (*U. S. Statistical Abstract* and *1937 Census of Manufactures*), on the basis of 1 cord of pulpwood = 90 cubic feet or 2.548 solid cubic meters; and 1 solid cubic meter of pulpwood = 530 kilograms (*Year-Book of World Timber Trade*, 1936, pp. 14, 15).

American experience, will suffice for present purposes. On this basis, the figures for 1937 indicate that net exports of woodpulp more than offset the area's net imports of timber, while in 1929 a very narrow export margin is shown. These comparisons are given in the accompanying table, page 77.

This table indicates, in a general way, the character of world trade in timber and woodpulp, and the part Europe played in this trade. It will be seen that roughly one-third of the world's timber exports, and more than half of the woodpulp exports, were from German-area countries, both in 1937 and in 1929. Strange as it may seem, the area was on an import basis for pulpwood. Such imports from outside sources, in fact, accounted for more than half the area's net exports of woodpulp.[8]

While all parts of the area have participated in the timber and woodpulp trades, a small number of states have accounted for the greater part of it. Sweden alone exported two-thirds of the woodpulp shipped from the area; France and Italy were the two big importers. Three countries—Sweden, Austria, and Poland—together accounted for well over half of the timber exports; Germany and the Netherlands were the big importers. The table on page 79 shows the import and export trade in timber and woodpulp, by countries.

The greater part of the export trade in timber has been intra-area in character, but woodpulp has gone principally to outside markets. Other states within the area took more than 55 per cent of the sawlogs and sawn and hewn timber shipped by Sweden, Austria, and Poland, the three big exporters. For the area as a whole, intra-area

---

[8] Practically all of these pulpwood imports came from the Russian area.

Timber and Woodpulp Trade, 1937, 1929[a]

Countries (By groups)	Timber (Thousand cubic meters)				Woodpulp (Thousand metric tons)			
	1937[b]		1929		1937[b]		1929	
	Imports	Exports	Imports	Exports	Imports	Exports	Imports	Exports
I. Bulgaria.........	6	—	180	—	11	—	—	—
Rumania........	6	1,732	50	1,940	—	8	—	—
Yugoslavia......	10	1,594	—	2,449	22	—	24	12
Total........	22	3,326	230	4,389	33	8	24	12
II. Denmark........	694	11	907	—	50	—	43	—
Hungary........	1,311	26	1,456	—	42	—	14	—
Netherlands.....	2,983	25	4,058	95	112	2	92	9
Poland..........	18	2,846	—	5,283	23	3	37	9
Portugal........	60	464	39	185	15	4	6	3
Spain...........	618	—	1,227	90	125	—	108	—
Total........	5,684	3,372	7,687	5,653	367	9	300	21
III. Albania.........	12	2	...	...	—	—	—	—
Greece..........	369	—	626	—	24	—	7	—
Norway.........	828	267	711	798	17	673	38	515
Sweden.........	550	4,721	353	7,067	12	2,553	—	1,789
Total........	1,759	4,990	1,690	7,865	53	3,226	45	2,304
IV. Germany........	7,541	78	10,973	1,420	185	166	164	277
Austria.........	52	2,854	137	3,037	4	186	5	113
Belgium-Luxemburg....	2,155	100	2,926	21	174	22	158	8
Czechoslovakia...	235	1,698	139	1,735	9	110	17	82
France..........	2,034	1,144	3,590	1,905	664	4	608	15
Italy...........	1,523	75	2,932	—	251	—	205	—
Switzerland......	312	37	804	—	21	7	15	10
Total........	13,852	5,986	21,501	8,118	1,308	495	1,172	505
All Nazi Europe......	21,317	17,674	31,108	26,025	1,761	3,738	1,541	2,842

[a] Compiled from sources cited in footnote *a* to table on p. 77. Timber trade includes sawn and hewn wood and logs for sawing, pit-props, railway ties, and pulpwood. Trade in woodpulp for 1937 and for exports in 1929 are in terms of dry pulp, but imports for 1929 are somewhat overstated since, in most cases, they were not reported in terms of dry pulp.
[b] Figures for Spain are for 1935, the latest available.

markets absorbed 57 per cent of the shipments of such timber. In the case of woodpulp, only 32 per cent of the export tonnage went to other countries inside the area— and roughly 27 per cent of the woodpulp from Sweden, the area's principal exporter. Practically all of the pulp-wood exports were retained in the area. The general character of the markets and sources of supply are shown by the table below, which covers about 90 per cent of the trade in timber (sawlogs, sawn and hewn timber, and pulpwood), and 93 per cent of the trade in woodpulp.

WHERE NAZI EUROPE BOUGHT AND SOLD TIMBER AND WOODPULP, 1937[a]

I. SAWLOGS, SAWN AND HEWN TIMBER, AND PULPWOOD
(In thousands of cubic meters)

Group	Exports to and Imports from Inside the Area			Exports to and Imports from Outside Countries		
	Exports	Imports	Net	Exports	Imports	Net
I........	1,470	—	−1,470	1,691	—	−1,691
II.......	1,077	2,233	+1,156	1,353	2,178	+ 825
III......	2,037	898	−1,139	2,632	837	−1,795
IV.......	4,750	6,203	+1,453	118	6,611	+6,493
Total...	9,334	9,334	0	5,794	9,626	+3,832

II. WOODPULP
(In thousands of metric tons)

I........	8	32	+ 24	—	2	+ 2
II.......	9	193	+ 184	—	50	+ 50
III......	844	34	− 810	2,382	18	−2,364
IV.......	326	928	+ 602	169	380	+ 211
Total...	1,187	1,187	0	2,551	450	−2,101

[a] Compiled from League of Nations, *International Trade in Certain Raw Materials and Foodstuffs*, 1938, except for pulpwood (included with timber), which was from Comité Internationale du Bois, *Year-Book of World Timber Trade*, 1938, and from official trade reports. Excludes the trade of Spain for which 1937 data were not available. For method used, see footnote *a* to table, p. 21.

Timber imports from outside sources have come principally from the Russian area. Finland, Russia, and Latvia together accounted for 43 per cent of the imports. French Equatorial Africa and French West Africa were the principal sources for hard woods.

Practically all of the woodpulp exports to outside markets have gone to the United States and the United Kingdom. These two countries alone took 2.2 million tons of the 2.5 millions shipped to all outside markets in 1937. Japan, the outside market of next importance, took only a small fraction of the total. The table below shows the principal European exporters and the outside markets for their product.

PRINCIPAL MARKETS FOR WOODPULP, 1937[a]
(In thousands of metric tons)

European Exporter	Exports to Outside Markets				
	Total	United States	United Kingdom	Japan	Other
Sweden............	1,854	1,025	577	124	128
Norway...........	474	93	310	63	8
Germany..........	104	63	20	.2	21
Czechoslovakia.....	44	35	3	4	2
Austria............	16	5	3	—	8
Belgium-Luxemburg.	6	—	6	—	—
Other area states...	22	12	7	.2	3
Total..........	2,520	1,233	926	191	170
WORLD EXPORTS....	4,744	2,173	1,825	474	272

[a] Compiled from data reported by the importing countries, as published by the League of Nations in *International Trade in Certain Raw Materials and Foodstuffs*, 1938.

Nazi Europe's timber shortage would be considerably increased if Mediterranean Asia and Africa were also in the area. Almost without exception, these Mediterranean countries were net importers of timber; and taken together, they had net imports equal to one-third those of Nazi Europe. So far as woodpulp is concerned, the inclusion of these countries would not change the position of the area, since none of them report any woodpulp (or pulpwood) production or trade. Figures covering timber trade are given on page 82, in thousands of cubic meters—the plus sign indicating net imports, the minus sign net exports.

	1937		1929	
Nazi Europe.................	+3,643		+5,083	
Mediterranean Africa:				
Algeria..................	+201		+ 345	
French Morocco...........	+ 98		+ 124	
Tunisia..................	+ 82		+ 81	
Egypt...................	+503		+1,007	
Libya...................	...		+ 14	
Spanish Morocco..........	...	+ 884	—	+1,571
Mediterranean Asia:				
Turkey..................	− 24		− 30	
Syria and Lebanon........	+102		+ 80	
Palestine................	+255		+ 75	
Cyprus..................	+ 28	+ 361	+ 17	+ 142
		+4,888		+6,796

Because there is no systematic and reliable compilation of production data with regard to timber, the foregoing analysis has necessarily been limited to a discussion of trade. What is needed is a measure of the annual growth of timber, and also of the amount cut each year. A combination of the figures for annual trade and annual timber cut would show total consumption, and indicate the relative importance of domestic and foreign sources of supply. A comparison of new timber growth with the amount cut would show the extent to which the area was building up or depleting its timber reserves. It is the opinion of experts in the timber trade that the countries of Europe have been heavily over-cutting their timber for a number of years.[9] If this is the case, then in the future Europe will have to restrict consumption or import increased amounts from outside sources.

[9] U. S. Dept. of Commerce, Forestry Products Division, *Recent World Trade Trends in Lumber and Timber Products* (January 1941).

SUMMARY

For most agricultural and forestry raw materials, the shortages shown by net imports have been somewhat larger for Nazi Europe than for the old Reich. The outstanding exceptions have been timber and woodpulp. In fact, in the case of woodpulp the German-controlled area has had a large volume of *exports*—as compared with small net *imports* into Germany alone. Timber imports for the 20 states combined are less than half those for Germany. A graphic comparison of the net trade of the two areas is given below in tonnage terms.

AGRICULTURAL AND FORESTRY RAW MATERIALS, 1937
Net Trade of Germany and Nazi Europe Compared

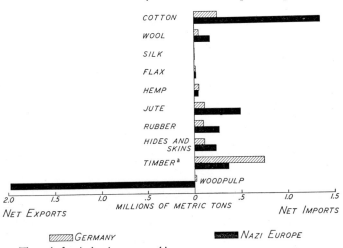

a The unit for timber is 10,000 cubic meters.

As percentages of total consumption, on the other hand, the net imports of Nazi Europe have been smaller than those for Germany—except in the case of two commodities. One of these was jute, of which there is no production on the whole continent of Europe; and the other was rubber, of which Germany had begun synthetic production as early as 1937, while no rubber production of any kind was reported for any other European country. But even so, the larger area is dependent on outside sources for a very considerable part of the agricultural and forestry materials it consumes. In the past, imports have accounted for practically all of the cotton and more than 70 per cent of the wool consumed in Nazi Europe, for about 40 per cent of the silk, 10 to 20 per cent of the flax, 15 per cent of the hemp, and all of the jute.

About half of the cotton imports came from the United States with the rest distributed among Brazil, India, Egypt, and small amounts from other countries. The greater part of the wool imports came from British Empire sources; and about 17 per cent from South American countries. Flax came from the Russian area; hemp from the Russian area, the Philippines, and China; and all of the jute consumed in the area was supplied by India. The rubber consumed in the area—aside from a relatively small amount of artificial rubber—came principally from British Malaya and the Dutch East Indies. A large share of the hides and skins came from Argentina and Brazil. Timber imports came principally from the Soviet states. Woodpulp was on an export basis, with practically all of the outgoing tonnage shipped to the United States and the United Kingdom.

CHAPTER IV

INDUSTRIAL MINERALS

A small number of industrial minerals accounts for most of the tonnage of such raw materials moving in world trade—principally iron and steel, coal, manganese, copper, lead, zinc, bauxite and aluminum, petroleum, and the three principal fertilizer materials, nitrate, phosphate, and potash. Various other minerals are of strategic importance in modern industry, but are produced and consumed in relatively small amounts.

For many of these subsoil products the old Reich was largely dependent on outside sources of supply, and the same is true with regard to the larger German area. In fact, existing shortages in many cases have actually been increased by the expansion into additional European territory. For other minerals, the larger area, like the old Reich, is on an export basis. However, to repeat what was said in Chapter II, it is only through foreign trade that a surplus of potash, for example, can be made to meet a shortage, say, in copper. In the present chapter, therefore, the problem of Nazi Europe's supply of each of the principal industrial minerals will be considered, with no attempt made to balance the exportable surpluses of some against deficiencies in others.[1]

[1] In this chapter, the text discussion is based in part on publications of the U. S. Bureau of Mines, as follows: *Mineral Raw Materials* (1937); *Minerals Yearbook*, 1940; *The Iron and Steel Industries of Europe*, Economic Paper 19 (1939); *Potash*, Economic Paper 16 (1933); *Foreign Minerals Quarterly*, various numbers; and *Coal Mining in Europe*, Bulletin 414 (1939). We have also drawn upon U. S. Tariff Commission, *Iron and Steel*, Report No. 128, 2d Series, 1938; 75 Cong. 3 sess., *Phosphate Resources of the U. S.*, Hearings on Public Resolution No. 112, before Joint Committee to Investigate the Adequacy and Use of Phosphate Resources of the U. S. (1939); and Donald Wilhelm, *The Book of Metals* (1932).

I. SHORTAGES OF MINERAL RAW MATERIALS

In the past, the area now under German control has fallen short of producing many of the important minerals in the volume required by its industries. These include copper, lead, zinc, petroleum, phosphorus, manganese, and a number of others that are consumed in smaller amounts but are of outstanding importance in modern industry.

A. Copper

Except for iron, copper is the world's most important industrial metal, accounting for over one-third of total consumption in the nonferrous metal industries. Its largest use—and the one for which it formerly was thought to be without a substitute—is in the electrical industries. For the past two decades, however, it has been replaced to an increasing extent by aluminum in countries lacking an adequate supply of copper—particularly in Germany.

Of the crude copper consumed in Nazi Europe, about 80 per cent is supplied from imported ore and metal. The table on page 87 gives figures regarding the trade and production of the several states of the area. Except for changes in the stock pile, the difference between smelter output and mine production gives a rough measure of the trade in ore,[2] while smelter output plus net imports of crude metal gives a measure of the crude metal consumed.

[2] Direct computation of the ore trade in terms of copper content is made difficult or impossible by the fact that (1) ores vary widely in copper content from one area to another, while ores, matte, and concentrates are reported together in many cases, so that the copper content of the "ores" group in the trade figures may vary from as low as 1½ or 2 per cent to as much as 50 per cent, with no rough average generally applicable to the trade, and that (2) about half of Nazi Europe's ore imports cannot be traced to country of origin, but in large part are imputed to countries that report neither production nor exports.

COPPER TRADE AND PRODUCTION, 1937, 1929[a]

[In thousands of metric tons; net imports (+), net exports (−)]

Countries (By groups)	1937			1929		
	Mine Production (Copper content)	Crude Shapes (Metal content)		Mine Production (Copper content)	Crude Shapes (Metal content)	
		Net Trade	Smelter Output		Net Trade	Smelter Output
I. Bulgaria......	—	+ .1	—	2.0	—	—
Rumania.....	1.4	+ 5.0	1.4	.1	...	.1
Yugoslavia....	42.3	− 36.3	39.4	15.2	− 18.7	20.7
Total.......	43.7	− 31.2	40.8	17.3	− 18.7	20.8
II. Denmark.....	—	+ 5.3	—	—	+ 1.3	—
Hungary......	.3	+ 12.0	—	—	+ 9.0	—
Netherlands	—	+ 5.3	—	—	+ 5.2	—
Poland.......	—	+ 17.9	—	—	+ 9.3	—
Portugal.....	5.6	+ 3.9	—	4.0	+ 2.3	—
Spain.........	28.0	+ 5.4[b]	10.2	63.7	− 20.3	28.5
Total.......	33.9	+ 49.8	10.2	67.7	+ 6.8	28.5
III. Albania.......	—	—	—	—	—	—
Greece........	.3	—	—	—	—	.5
Norway......	20.1	− 8.6	8.3	18.9	− 2.8	2.4
Sweden.......	7.2	+ 37.9	9.1	1.1	+ 17.4	4.7
Total.......	27.6	+ 29.3	17.4	20.0	+ 14.6	7.6
IV. Germany.....	30.4	+195.5	65.5	29.0	+185.1	53.6
Austria.......	—	+ 18.2	2.1	2.1	+ 13.8	3.9
Belgium-Luxembourg..	—	+ 9.6	90.3[c]	—	+ 59.6	8.9
Czechoslovakia	.7	+ 30.5	2.0	1.4	+ 14.1	1.7
France.......	.6	+119.2	1.0	.6	+157.6	1.0
Italy.........	1.1	+ 76.6	1.5	.9	+ 54.4	.5
Switzerland...	—	+ 19.3	—	—	+ 13.9	—
Total.......	32.8	+468.9	162.4	34.0	+498.5	69.6
All Nazi Europe...	138.0	+516.8	230.8	139.0	+501.2	126.5

[a] Production data are from U. S. Bureau of Mines, *Minerals Yearbook*, 1934 and 1940, and from League of Nations, *Statistical Year-book*, 1938–39, and 1939–40. Net imports are from official trade reports, and from Imperial Institute, *The Mineral Industry of the British Empire and Foreign Countries*, *Statistical Summary*, 1928–1930, and 1936–1938. Trade data for crude copper include ingots, pigs, slabs, cathodes, and other crude forms, and waste and scrap material. Copper recovered from domestic supplies of scrap and waste is not accounted for in smelter output.

[b] Net trade for Spain is for 1935 since 1937 data are not available.

[c] Metallgesellschaft, *Metal Statistics*, 1929–1938, p. 10, reports smelter output excluding that from Belgian Congo matte as 8,000 metric tons.

Yugoslavia, Spain, Norway, and Germany are all producers of ore. German production, however, is on a high-cost basis from mines that are nearing commercial exhaustion. The principal smelter capacity of the area is in Germany and Belgium—capacity in the latter country having been increased in recent years to parallel the expansion in mine output from the Belgian Congo.

Well over half of Nazi Europe's imports of crude copper has come from the Western Hemisphere. Figures for 1937 covering 488,900 metric tons from outside sources and

PRINCIPAL OUTSIDE SOURCES FOR CRUDE COPPER, 1937, 1929[a]
(In thousands of metric tons)

Exporting Area	1937			1929		
	Exports to Nazi Europe	Total Exports	Production (Smelter output)	Exports to Nazi Europe	Total Exports	Production (Smelter output)
Western Hemisphere:						
United States...	149.2	286.7	820.3	265.4	392.6	998.8
Chile...........	130.7	384.9	396.4	90.1	308.3	303.2
Canada.........	21.0	141.8	210.0	8.0	72.5	72.7
Three countries	300.9	813.4	1,426.7	363.5	773.4	1,374.7
Africa:						
Belgian Congo...	84.5	84.5	97.3	90.9	122.6	135.5
British Africa...	67.1	211.1	224.8	5.3	13.5	15.3
Two areas....	151.6	295.6	322.1	96.2	136.1	150.8
United Kingdom...	36.4[b]	26.3	7.5	25.1[b]	18.3	22.0
Total for sources listed..........	488.9	1,135.3	1,756.3	484.8	927.8	1,547.5
WORLD TOTAL[c].....	724.8	1,566.0	2,345.0	647.7	1,283.0	1,904.0

[a] Data are from sources listed in footnote *a*, table on p. 87, and from *Statistisches Jahrbuch fuer das Deutsche Reich*, 1938.

[b] U. K. exports to Nazi Europe, as shown by reports of the importing countries, are larger than total exports as reported by Britain.

[c] Trade figures include the intra-area trade of Nazi Europe—amounting to 165,100 metric tons in 1937, and 125,100 tons in 1929.

165,100 tons of intra-area trade (or 90 per cent of the total "import" trade) show that 301,000 were from the United States, Chile, and Canada. In 1929, a somewhat larger proportion of imports was shipped from Western Hemisphere countries. This is shown by the accompanying table.

The table also shows that this trade was a matter of considerable importance to the principal producing countries. Shipments to Nazi Europe have accounted for over half of all copper exports from the United States; for one-third of Chilean exports and Chilean production; for practically all of the output from the Belgian Congo; and for roughly one-third of the rapidly expanding supply produced in British Africa.

No appreciable change in the area's copper resources would result from annexation of Mediterranean Asia and Africa. The only copper producer in this south Mediterranean area is the Island of Cyprus, whose mines of the red metal are known to date back as early as 3000 B.C.[3] In 1937 shipments of ore from the Island amounted to less than 4 per cent of Nazi Europe's consumption of crude copper, and in 1929 to approximately 1 per cent. This is indicated by the summary statement below, which shows the area's mine production and apparent consumption of crude copper, in comparison with the total output of the Island. Figures are in thousands of metric tons, copper content.

	1937	1929
Mine production of Nazi Europe............	138.0	139.0
Ore shipments from Cyprus................	27.5	5.9
Total, Nazi Europe and Cyprus............	165.5	144.9
Nazi Europe's apparent consumption of crude copper shapes.........................	747.6	627.7

[3] Ira B. Joralemon, *Romantic Copper* (1935), p. 6.

Other countries in the south Mediterranean group reported some trade in rough and scrap copper, but in negligible quantities. In 1937 this trade showed net imports of less than 1,000 metric tons, and in 1929 less than 4,000.

Taken as a whole, net imports of copper have represented about 80 per cent of copper consumption in Nazi Europe alone, and also in Nazi Europe combined with the Mediterranean group of countries.

B. Lead

Lead is an indispensable raw material for many industries. Because it resists corrosion and is a nonconductor of electricity, it is used as a covering for overhead, underground, and underwater cables. It has no known substitute for use in the manufacture of storage batteries—and therefore is of vital importance in the manufacture of automobiles, farm tractors, and all other types of automotive vehicles and machinery. Neither has it any substitute for use as a type metal. It is also important in the manufacture of paint and in the production of antiknock gasoline, and is consumed in large quantities in many other industries.

Around 50 per cent of Europe's requirements for newly mined lead are supplied from imports of ore and crude metal. Germany, the world's third largest consumer of this metal (following the United States and the United Kingdom), imported two-thirds of her supply; and France, the second largest consumer in Europe, was almost entirely dependent on imports. The trade and production of the area are shown by the table on page 91.

The countries of Europe with the largest mine production, as shown by the table, are Germany, Yugoslavia, and Spain. The last of these was by far the largest producer in the area until her mines were badly damaged during the recent civil war—with the result that output was decreased by 50 per cent from 1929 to 1935, and was again cut in half by 1937.

LEAD TRADE AND PRODUCTION, 1937, 1929[a]

(In thousands of metric tons)

Countries (By groups)	1937[b]				1929			
	Ore (Lead content)		Pig Lead		Ore (Lead content)		Pig Lead	
	Net Trade[c]	Mine Production	Net Trade[c] (Including scrap)	Smelter Output	Net Trade[c]	Mine Production	Net Trade[c] (Including scrap)	Smelter Output
I. Bulgaria.....	—	.2	+ .5	—	− 1.9	3.7	+ .4	—
Rumania....	—	7.4	− .1	7.5	− 2.6[d]	—	+ 2.3[d]	0.6
Yugoslavia..	− 68.7	71.0	− 2.5	4.0	− 1.7	14.7	+ .1	9.5
Total.....	− 68.7	78.6	− 2.1	11.5	− 6.2	18.4	+ 2.8	10.1
II. Denmark....	—	—	+ 7.8	—	—	—	+ 5.6	—
Hungary....	—	—	+ 6.1	.1	—	—	+ 4.5	.1
Netherlands.	+ .1	—	+ 20.4	—	—	—	+ 19.9	—
Poland......	+ .9	6.2	+ .5	17.6	+ 12.2	11.6	− 13.2	35.8
Portugal....	—	1.3	+ 2.3	—	+ .3	.2	—	.1
Spain.......	− .4	66.2	− 43.2	70.6	− 2.5	116.5	− 99.4	142.8
Total.....	+ .6	73.7	− 6.1	88.3	+ 9.4	128.3	− 82.6	178.8
III. Albania.....	—	—	—	—	—	—	—	—
Greece......	—	8.5	− 2.2	9.2	− 2.2	4.2	+ 1.0	5.4
Norway.....	− .2	.4	+ 3.0	.2	—	—	+ .9	—
Sweden	− 9.6	9.3	+ 17.9	—	− 6.8	7.0	+ 7.2	—
Total.....	− 9.8	18.2	+ 18.7	9.4	− 9.0	11.2	+ 9.1	5.4
IV. Germany....	+ 76.8	78.9	+ 72.9	166.4	+ 32.7	60.5	+114.4	97.9
Austria......	+ 4.2	8.7	− 4.3	10.8	+ .9	7.5	+ 8.0	6.6
Belgium-Luxemburg	+ 79.6	—	− 38.5	84.8	+ 19.7	—	+ 10.8	60.0
Czecho-slovakia...	—	3.9	+ 14.6	5.1	− .4	4.5	+ 12.7	4.6
France......	+ 20.0	4.6	+ 71.3	38.2	+ 7.1	11.2	+ 92.0	20.4
Italy........	+ 4.8	35.0	+ 11.1	39.5	− 4.5	30.5	+ 24.6	22.7
Switzerland..	− .2	—	+ 9.0	—	− .2	—	+ 10.5	—
Total.....	+185.2	131.1	+136.1	344.8	+ 55.3	114.2	+273.0	212.2
All Nazi Europe...	+107.3	301.6	+146.6	454.0	+ 49.5	272.1	+202.3	406.5

[a] Mine production and smelter output from League of Nations, *Statistical Year-book*, 1938–39 and 1939–40. Trade data are from sources listed in footnote *a*, p. 87. Smelter production does not include lead recovered from scrap or waste materials.

[b] Figures for Spain are for 1935 since complete data are not available for 1937.

[c] Net imports (+), net exports (−).

[d] Net imports for Rumania are for 1930, since data are not available for 1929.

As much as two-thirds of the lead imported from outside the area has come from the Western Hemisphere. Imports came principally from Mexico in 1937, while in 1929 the largest imports were from the United States, Australia, and Mexico—in order of importance. The accompanying table shows shipments of lead to Nazi Europe in comparison with the total exports and production of the principal outside sources of supply. It will be seen that Nazi Europe took about half of Mexico's total exports and production in 1937, and practically all of the smaller amounts produced in French North Africa and Turkey.

PRINCIPAL OUTSIDE SOURCES FOR LEAD, 1937, 1929[a]
(Amounts are in thousands of metric tons, lead content)

Exporting Area	1937				1929			
	Exports to Nazi Europe		Total Exports (Including ore)	Production of Lead Ore	Exports to Nazi Europe		Total Exports (Including ore)	Production of Lead Ore
	Ore	Pig Lead and Scrap			Ore	Pig Lead and Scrap		
Western Hemisphere:								
Mexico..........	—	117.3	245.9	218.1	—	48.6	236.6	248.4
Canada and Newfoundland.......	24.6	5.1	187.8	216.1	10.7	10.2	117.9	159.1
Peru.............	15.9	8.3	38.7	42.0	2.0	—	21.8	21.4
Bolivia...........	14.8	—	18.3	18.3	3.5	—	14.9	15.0
United States......	—	8.6	18.2	421.7	.9	56.2	65.5	590.0
Argentina........	4.5	—	5.9	15.0	2.8	—	.1	2.9
Six areas........	59.8	139.3	514.8	931.2	19.9	115.0	456.8	1,036.8
French North Africa..	7.9	21.8	41.5	33.4	11.3	17.1	31.7	29.9
Australia...........	14.7	8.6	223.4	250.0	5.4	48.2	167.0	197.1
United Kingdom.....	5.1	16.2	12.2	26.8	4.4	5.7	12.7	18.9
Turkey.............	5.2	—	4.4	4.8	—	8.4	2.8	5.1
British India (Burma)	—	.5	85.9	92.7	.3	17.1	84.3	103.7
Total all sources listed	92.7	186.4	882.2	1,338.9	41.3	211.5	755.3	1,391.5
WORLD TOTAL[b].......	194.5	281.8	1,115.4	1,697.0	97.3	365.5	981.3	1,715.0

[a] Production data are from League of Nations, *Statistical Year-book*, 1938–39 and 1939–40. Trade data are from sources listed in footnote *a*, table, p. 87.
[b] Trade figures include intra-area trade of Nazi Europe (in thousands of metric tons, lead content) as follows: 86.2 in ore and 82.4 in pig lead and scrap for 1937; 44.0 in ore and 132.5 in pig lead and scrap for 1929.

If the Mediterranean countries were included in the German area, its dependence on foreign lead would remain practically unchanged. In normal years, only four of these countries report any trade in lead ore, and none of them take part in the pig lead trade. Net exports from all four of these ore-trading countries, taken together, would have supplied Nazi Europe with only 2 per cent of consumption requirements in both years studied here. The trade of these countries is shown below, in thousands of metric tons, with the plus sign indicating net imports and the minus sign net exports.[4]

	1937	1929
Ore trade (lead content):		
Algeria	− 3.5	−7.8
French Morocco	− 8.3	−2.5
Tunisia	+ 4.0	+2.9
Turkey	− 4.2	−2.3
Total	−12.0	−9.7

Some trade in lead metal was reported by six of the Mediterranean countries, but the amounts involved were very small, except in the case of Tunisia. In the aggregate this trade showed net exports of 23,200 metric tons in 1937, and 14,600 in 1929.[5]

C. Zinc

World production of lead and zinc are about equal in amount, and taken together they account for almost half of the metal tonnage consumed in the nonferrous industries. In its principal uses zinc is combined with other metals: about 40 per cent of the annual supply is used as coating for other metals (galvanized iron, etc.), and almost 30 per cent is alloyed with copper to make brass. Smaller amounts are consumed in die castings, in rolled zinc, and various other uses.

About 80 per cent of Nazi Europe's consumption of new zinc is from domestic mines, and 20 per cent from outside sources. The area is a large net importer of ore. But with a smelter capacity in excess of domestic requirements

[4] Compiled from publications of the Imperial Institute.
[5] Net exports from Tunisia amounted to 24,000 metric tons in 1937 and 18,200 in 1929, offset in both years by small net imports for some of the other Mediterranean countries.

for the crude metal, it is a net exporter of slab zinc. A few countries have had mine production in excess of domestic consumption. Poland and Belgium-Luxemburg, in particular, have had excess smelter capacity—that of Poland being in good working order when the Germans

ZINC TRADE AND PRODUCTION, 1937, 1929[a]

(In thousands of metric tons)

Countries (By groups)	1937[b]				1929			
	Ore (Zinc content)		Slab Zinc		Ore (Zinc content)		Slab Zinc	
	Net Trade[c]	Mine Production	Net Trade[c] (Including scrap)	Smelter Output	Net Trade[c]	Mine Production	Net Trade[c] (Including scrap)	Smelter Output
I. Bulgaria.....	—	—	+ 1.2	—	—	—	+ .9	—
Rumania....	− 7.6	6.3	+ 5.4	6.3	− 3.6	1.1	+ 2.3[d]	—
Yugoslavia..	− 32.2	48.8	− 1.9	4.3	+ 9.3	0.5	− 4.1	6.3
Total.....	− 39.8	55.1	+ 4.7	10.6	+ 5.7	1.6	− .9	6.3
II. Denmark....	—	—	+ 3.4	—	—	—	+ 2.0	—
Hungary....	—	—	+ 6.3	—	—	—	+ 5.4	—
Netherlands.	+ 25.7	—	− 17.9	24.6	+ 38.9	—	− 19.3	25.7
Poland......	+ 34.5[e]	72.0	− 74.7	107.2	+102.9	105.0	−139.8	169.0
Portugal....	—	—	—	—	—	—	—	—
Spain.......	− 39.6	20.0	− .2	5.3	− 48.7	53.0	− 2.6	11.8
Total.....	+ 20.6	92.0	− 83.1	137.1	+ 93.1	158.0	−154.3	206.5
III. Albania.....	—	—	—	—	—	—	—	—
Greece......	—	10.9	+ .9	—	− .4	5.9	+ .1	—
Norway.....	+ 29.7	8.8	− 36.7	41.3	+ 8.1	1.4	− 2.0	5.5
Sweden.....	− 35.7	36.0	+ 14.0	—	− 34.1	29.9	+ 3.4	4.7
Total.....	− 6.0	55.7	− 21.8	41.3	− 26.4	37.2	+ 1.5	10.2
IV. Germany....	+ 24.3	165.6	+ 70.5	163.3	+ 1.1	142.5	+ 94.3	102.0
Austria......	− 2.7	3.0	+ 8.1	—	− 2.0	4.0	+ 6.2	—
Belgium-Luxemburg	+272.9	3.0	−131.7	217.8	+287.4	5.0	− 64.6	197.9
Czecho-slovakia...	+ 9.0	2.0	+ 9.9	7.2	+ 9.4	—	+ 15.4	10.7
France......	+ 49.0	.9	+ 34.3	56.6	+103.5	9.9	+ 23.4	87.3
Italy........	− 37.4	80.0	+ .1	38.0	− 81.2	87.0	+ 7.1	15.8
Switzerland..	—	—	+ 7.8	—	—	—	+ 3.6	—
Total.....	+315.1	254.5	− 1.0	482.9	+318.2	248.4	+ 85.4	413.7
All Nazi Europe...	+289.9	457.3	−101.2	671.9	+390.6	445.2	− 68.3	636.7

[a] Mine production and smelter output compiled from League of Nations, *Statistical Yearbook* 1938–39 and 1939–40. Trade data are from sources listed in footnote *a*, p. 87.
[b] Trade data for Spain are for 1935 since 1937 data were not available.
[c] Net imports (+), net exports (−).
[d] Trade data for Rumania are for 1930 since 1929 data were not available.
[e] Polish ore imports were mainly "blende" (67 per cent zinc content); the only data on ore exports for 1937 were from the German import statistics, which indicated receipts of "tailings" (low grade ore, semi-waste) from Poland amounting to 47,500 metric tons. Other ore exports estimated from comparison of mine output and smelter production.

invaded the country and appropriated these properties. Germany, the largest producer and consumer in the area, supplies more than 70 per cent of her requirements from domestic mines. The trade and production of the area are shown by the preceding table, page 94.

In the aggregate, Nazi Europe has produced about 25 per cent of the world's annual supply of new zinc, and consumed more than 30 per cent. Its production of new zinc has been considerably less, but its consumption about the same as that of the United States—the world's largest producer and consumer of the metal.

PRINCIPAL OUTSIDE SOURCES FOR ZINC, 1937, 1929[a]
(Amounts are in thousands of metric tons, zinc content)

Exporting Area	1937				1929			
	Exports to Nazi Europe		Total Exports (Including ore)	Total Mine Production	Exports to Nazi Europe		Total Exports (Including ore)	Total Mine Production
	Ore	Slab Zinc and Scrap			Ore	Slab Zinc and Scrap		
Western Hemisphere:								
Mexico............	113.2	11.7	150.8	154.6	120.6	—	174.0	174.1
Canada and New-foundland.......	44.1	6.3	209.1	232.2	18.7	15.8	82.0	112.5
Peru.............	8.7	—	16.0	18.3	7.0	—	11.8	12.4
United States......	—	6.6[b]	2.4	568.2	6.8	11.7	17.3	657.2
Bolivia...........	6.6	—	11.5	11.5	2.4	—	1.4	1.4
Argentina.........	2.9	—	4.2	6.3	—	.4	.8	—
Six countries....	175.5	24.6	394.0	991.1	155.5	27.9	287.3	957.6
Australasia:								
British India (Burma)........	45.6	—	49.0	59.5	33.8	.1	34.3	56.3
Australia..........	37.8	.3	87.7	206.7	50.6	9.0	94.1	157.0
Turkey...........	10.1	—	12.6	10.0	2.1	.2	3.7	6.2
French Indo-China.	—	4.0	4.0	5.0	9.4	—	19.3	18.8
Four countries...	93.5	4.3	153.3	281.2	95.9	9.3	151.4	238.3
French North Africa..	15.5	—	30.0	14.1	15.8	.2	19.1	18.6
United Kingdom.....	10.3	2.3	19.0	7.7	9.6	2.8	15.2	.9
Total for sources listed	294.8	31.2	596.3	1,294.1	276.8	40.2	473.0	1,215.4
WORLD TOTAL[c].......	584.1	213.5	1,218.1	1,870.0	695.1	248.1	1,139.2	1,713.0

[a] Exports to Nazi Europe compiled from official import statistics of the importing countries. Total exports and production are from sources listed in footnote *a*, p. 87.
[b] According to *Metallgesellschaft*, "... possibly include certain quantities of Mexican spelter."
[c] Trade figures include intra-area trade of Nazi Europe as follows (in thousands of metric tons): zinc in ore 255.6, and metallic zinc 163.1, in 1937; zinc in ore 314.7, and metallic zinc 200.1, in 1929.

A large part of the zinc ore imported from outside sources came from Western Hemisphere countries. Australasia supplied most of the remainder. Mexico was the outstanding single source of supply. Shipments from one part of the area to another accounted for a large share of the total import trade, but these cancel out in the figures for net trade. The accompanying table shows the sources of imports, and compares the amounts taken from each source with the total exports and mine production of the exporting countries.

In both years covered by the table, exports from the United States to Europe were very small. British India sent a large proportion of her output to Europe. Both Australia and Canada, the other important producing countries in the British Empire, sold zinc in Europe but found their principal markets elsewhere.

The Mediterranean area is a net exporter of zinc, but in relatively small amounts. Four of these countries reported net exports of zinc ore in 1937, and only three in 1929. Figures for this trade are given below—in thousands of metric tons, all of them with minus signs, indicating net exports.[6]

	1937	1929
Ore trade (zinc content):		
Algeria	− 8.9	−14.0
French Morocco	− 3.9	—
Tunisia	− 2.0	− 3.0
Turkey	−12.5	− 3.2
Total	−27.3	−20.2

There was also a very small trade in rough and scrap zinc, figures for all reporting countries showing net imports of 1,500 metric tons in 1937, and net exports of 400 metric tons in 1929.

It will be seen that with the Mediterranean countries

[6] Compiled from publications of the Imperial Institute

included in the area, Nazi Europe would still be a net importer of zinc.

D. Petroleum

Petroleum provides the chief fuel for motor transportation, and the greater part of the lubricants used throughout the world. In many other uses it competes with natural gas, coal, and hydroelectric power.

Nazi Europe has depended on imports for roughly 60 per cent of the petroleum consumed in the area. However, such a comparison of imports and consumption is altogether inadequate for picturing the area's lack of this strategic mineral, for consumption has been very meager, particularly when compared with the levels to which we are accustomed. The area's poverty is better shown by the fact that, taken as a whole, it produces only 3 per cent of the world's annual total and consumes less than 8 per cent—while the United States produces 61 per cent, and consumes approximately 55 per cent. The trade and production of the area are shown by the table on page 98.

Rumania is the only area country whose crude production is of any moment. Her output, however, is a mere "drop of oil on a hot stove" in comparison with Germany's present war needs, and would fall considerably short of providing the United States with a two-week supply at our present rate of consumption. German and Polish production, taken together, amounted to less than one-half of 1 per cent of the world total. Consumption was largest in France, where a policy was followed of importing crude oil, to be processed in domestic refineries.

With account taken of benzol, synthetic gasoline, and natural gasoline, the area's 1937 production is raised from the 8.3 million metric tons shown in the table on

PETROLEUM TRADE AND PRODUCTION, 1937, 1929[a]
(In thousands of metric tons)

Countries (By groups)	1937[b]		1929	
	Net Imports (+) Net Exports (−)	Production of Crude Petroleum[c]	Net Imports (+) Net Exports (−)	Production of Crude Petroleum[c]
I. Bulgaria............	+ 88	—	+ 85	—
Rumania...........	− 5,163	7,150	−2,820	4,837
Yugoslavia.........	+ 113	—	+ 137	—
Total...........	− 4,962	7,150	−2,598	4,837
II. Denmark...........	+ 800	—	+ 471	—
Hungary...........	+ 280	2	+ 205	—
Netherlands........	+ 1,462	—	+ 950	—
Poland.............	− 78	501	− 176	675
Portugal...........	+ 194	—	+ 111	—
Spain..............	+ 222	—	+ 456	5
Total...........	+ 2,880	503	+2,017	680
III. Albania............	− 56	88	—	—
Greece.............	+ 322	—	+ 149	—
Norway............	+ 540	—	+ 270	—
Sweden............	+ 1,145	—	+ 435	—
Total...........	+ 1,951	88	+ 854	—
IV. Germany...........	+ 3,717	451	+2,241	103
Austria.............	+ 320	33	+ 229	—
Belgium-Luxemburg.	+ 486	—	+ 424	—
Czechoslovakia......	+ 458	18	+ 348	14
France.............	+ 7,221	79	+2,886	80
Italy...............	+ 2,442	16	+1,266	8
Switzerland........	+ 411	—	259	—
Total...........	+15,055	597	+7,653	205
All Nazi Europe.........	+14,924	8,338	+7,926	5,722

[a] Production data are from League of Nations, *Statistical Year-book*, 1938–39 and 1939–40. Trade data are from sources listed in footnote *a*, p. 87. Net imports cover the following products: crude petroleum, gasoline, kerosene, fuel oil and similar oils, and lubricating oils. Production of benzol, synthetic gasoline, and natural gasoline are not included. Exports of bunker oils, amounting to 2,294,000 tons in 1937, and 608,000 tons in 1929, have not been included in the computation of net trade.

According to the U. S. Department of Commerce, 1 metric ton of crude petroleum, on the average, equals slightly more than 7 barrels (of 42 American gallons each).

[b] Figures for Spain are for 1935 since 1937 data are not available.

[c] Includes oil from shale and asphalt rock.

page 98 to 10.5 millions. Consumption is increased from 23.2 millions to 25.4 millions. And with these motor fuels included, production represents only 40 per cent of consumption. Germany has been the only important producer of synthetic gasoline in the area, accounting for about 950,000 metric tons out of the 966,000 total reported for 1937—all of which was produced by the hydrogenation of coal. (A large new plant that is scheduled to start operation early in 1941 will use both coal and oil residues—the latter obtained in part from imports—as raw materials.) In 1937 Germany also accounted for 529,000 metric tons of benzol (a by-product of the coking industry) out of the area's 815,500 total. Rumania and Poland are producers of natural gasoline, their combined output in 1937 amounting to 347,000 metric tons.

Western Hemisphere countries provided about 60 per cent of the petroleum imported from all outside sources. Shipments from the United States were larger than from any other single source. They accounted for about 22 per cent of this country's total exports in 1937 but only a small fraction of total production. Soviet Russia, the world's second largest producer, consumed most of her output at home, and shipped only a small fraction to other countries in Europe. Further information regarding the sources of imports are given in the accompanying table, on page 100.

Exports from Venezuela—including direct shipments, and those going via the big refineries in the Dutch West Indies—accounted for about 14 per cent of that country's total production. The recently developed oil fields of Iraq shipped almost 80 per cent of their output to Europe, most of it going to French refineries. Smaller amounts were imported from other countries, though in some cases they represented a substantial fraction of the producing area's total output.

PRINCIPAL OUTSIDE SOURCES FOR PETROLEUM, 1937, 1929[a]
(In thousands of metric tons)

Exporting Area	1937			1929		
	Exports to Nazi Europe	Total Exports	Crude Petroleum Production	Exports to Nazi Europe	Total Exports	Crude Petroleum Production
Western Hemisphere:						
United States....	4,926	22,071	172,866	4,469	19,794	138,104
Dutch West Indies[b].........	3,019	20,155	—	500	11,446	—
Venezuela[b]......	912	25,965	27,734	612	19,262	19,845
Peru.............	615	2,016	2,309	48	1,508	1,777
Colombia.......	506	2,546	2,831	37	2,577	2,911
Mexico.........	470	3,000	7,159	417	3,508	6,700
Six countries..	10,448	75,753	212,899	6,083	58,095	169,337
Asia:						
Iraq............	3,413	4,180	4,255	36	...	121
Iran............	1,284	8,031	10,331	795	5,321	5,549
Dutch East Indies	244	5,461	7,262	29	3,488	5,239
Three countries	4,941	17,672	21,848	860	8,809	10,909
Russia...........	776	1,930	27,821	1,425	3,857	14,477
United Kingdom...	714	526	126[c]	497	430	169[c]
Total for sources listed.........	16,879	95,881	262,694	8,865	71,191	194,892
WORLD TOTAL[d].....	21,512	108,596	279,874	11,095	77,191	205,897

[a] Trade figures cover the commodities listed in footnote *a*, p. 98. Exports to Nazi Europe were compiled from official trade reports of the importing countries of Europe. Other data were compiled from *Statistisches Jahrbuch fuer das Deutsche Reich*, 1938; from League of Nations, *International Trade Statistics*, 1938, and *Statistical Year-book*, 1938-39 and 1939-40; and from Imperial Institute, *The Mineral Industry of the British Empire and Foreign Countries*, Statistical Summary, 1936-1938, and 1929-1931.

[b] Most of the Venezuelan crude oil goes to Netherlands West Indies (Curacao and Aruba) for refining.

[c] Shale oil; no crude petroleum is produced in the United Kingdom.

[d] Trade includes intra-area trade amounting to 3,589,000 tons in 1937 and 1,997,000 tons in 1929.

Increased imports of petroleum would be required if the Mediterranean group of countries were included in the area. Egypt, the only Mediterranean producer of any moment, supplied about 20 per cent of consumption requirements from domestic resources in 1937. The rest of the group depend on imports for all or for practically all of their supplies. The petroleum trade of these countries, together with that of Nazi Europe, is summarized below, in thousands of metric tons.

Territory	1937 (Net imports)		1929 (Net imports)	
Nazi Europe..........................		14,924		7,926
Mediterranean Africa:				
Algeria............................	248		172	
French Morocco...................	138		95	
Tunisia...........................	108		80	
Egypt............................	661		794	
Libya............................	49		9	
Spanish Morocco..................	8	1,212	...	1,150
Mediterranean Asia:				
Turkey...........................	134		98	
Syria and Lebanon................	90		69	
Palestine.........................	183		50	
Cyprus...........................	27	434	11	228
Total............................		16,570		9,304

Taken as a whole, the net imports of the Mediterranean group were about one-eighth as large as those of Nazi Europe in 1937, and about one-sixth as large in 1929. Annexed to Europe, therefore, these countries would add to the difficulties already faced with regard to oil. However, possession of these countries would open the gates south to Iraq and Iran (see table, page 100), countries whose exports in 1937 were almost as large as Nazi Europe's net imports from all outside sources of supply.

E. Phosphate

Phosphorus, one of the three elements essential for plant life, is likely to be lacking in soils that have long been used for wheat, oats, and various other crops, and must be replaced in the form of fertilizers. It is of particular importance for the growing of forage crops, increasing both their yield and their quality. Something like 90 per cent of the world's annual consumption is in the form of fertilizer materials. The rest goes into baking powder, dye manufactures, ferrophosphates used in making steel, etc.; and in wartime it is used in the manufacture of smoke screens, and phosphine gas. World production is principally from phosphate rock, and basic slag—a by-product of the iron industry. A small proportion comes from guano, bones, and various other organic materials.

Nazi Europe produces only 40 per cent of the phosphate consumed in the area. Practically all of the domestic product is from Germany, Belgium-Luxemburg, and France, and practically all of it is a by-product from the smelters that process the iron ores of the region, that have a high phosphorous content. Data showing trade and production in the European area are given on the opposite page.

French North Africa supplied around 45 to 50 per cent of the area's phosphate requirements. The United States was second in importance as a source of supply, furnishing almost 10 per cent of the amounts consumed in 1937 and 1929. Recently discovered deposits in Russia accounted for most of the remainder in 1937. The table on page 104 shows imports into Nazi Europe from the principal sources of supply in comparison with the latter's total exports and production.

PHOSPHATE TRADE AND PRODUCTION, 1937, 1929[a]
(In thousands of metric tons of P_2O_5)

Countries (By groups)	1937		1929	
	Net Imports[b]	Production	Net Imports[b]	Production
I. Bulgaria..............	—	—	—	—
Rumania.............	—	—	3	—
Yugoslavia...........	2	—	16	—
Total..............	2	—	19	—
II. Denmark.............	71	—	85	—
Hungary.............	8	—	27	—
Netherlands..........	132	—	137	—
Poland and Danzig....	52	2	112	7
Portugal.............	44	—	40	—
Spain...............	54	—	191	3
Total..............	361	2	592	10
III. Albania.............	—	—	—	—
Greece..............	13	—	1	—
Norway.............	17	—	12	—
Sweden.............	57	2	34	2
Total..............	87	2	47	2
IV. Germany............	419	370	434	302
Austria..............	14	—	15	—
Belgium-Luxemburg...	−85	233	−115	285
Czechoslovakia.......	26	26	56	24
France..............	217	262	245	435
Italy................	297	—	240	—
Switzerland..........	29	—	19	—
Total..............	917	891	894	1,046
All Nazi Europe...........	1,367	895	1,552	1,058

[a] Production data include phosphate rock and basic slag; trade includes the same and also superphosphates. Compiled from the following sources: *Superphosphate*, January and February 1939, December 1931, and February 1933; International Institute of Agriculture, *International Yearbook of Agricultural Statistics*, 1931–32 and 1938–39; U. S. Bureau of Mines, *Minerals Yearbook*, 1940; and League of Nations, *Statistical Year-book*, 1938–39. Phosphoric acid (P_2O_5) content was computed from percentages given in sources cited above—ranging from 17 to 40 per cent for phosphate rock; from 14 to 20 per cent for superphosphates; and from 14 to 23 per cent for basic slag. Guano and other organic phosphates are not included.

[b] Net exports (−).

PRINCIPAL OUTSIDE SOURCES FOR PHOSPHATE, 1937, 1929[a]
(Amounts are in thousands of metric tons of P_2O_5)

Exporting Area	1937			1929		
	Exports to Nazi Europe	Total Exports	Pro-duction	Exports to Nazi Europe	Total Exports	Pro-duction
French North Africa:						
Tunisia.............	439	540	496	628	845	703
Morocco............	445	535	479	417	552	578
Algeria.............	125	171	184	187	240	217
Total.............	1,009	1,246	1,159	1,319[b]	1,637	1,498
United States........	215	366	1,429	241	397	1,281
Russia..............	166	187	684[c]	—	—	38
Egypt...............	34	134	155	11	65	65
Total for sources listed............	1,424	1,933	3,427	1,571	2,099	2,882
WORLD TOTAL[d]........	1,798	3,083	5,094[e]	2,179	3,155	4,457[e]

[a] Exports to Nazi Europe were compiled from official trade reports of the importing countries and from 75 Cong. 3 sess., *Phosphate Resources of the U. S.*, Hearings on Public Resolution No. 112, before Joint Committee to Investigate the Adequacy and Use of Phosphate Resources of the U. S (1939). Other data are from sources cited in footnote *a*, p. 103.

[b] This total includes an additional 87,000 tons from French North Africa, not distributed by countries.

[c] Estimate based on 1935–36 production.

[d] Trade figures include intra-area trade amounting to 307,000 tons in 1937 and 551,000 tons in 1929.

[e] Includes P_2O_5 in basic slag, 932,000 tons in 1937, and 1,028,000 tons in 1929.

Nazi Europe has absorbed most of the world's exports of phosphate. However, in 1937 the two big producing countries, the United States and Soviet Russia, consumed considerably more at home than they exported. This was also true of the United States in 1929, when Russian production was still a negligible quantity. For the French colonies of North Africa, on the other hand, exports to the German area have accounted for almost all of the phosphate produced.

By acquiring control over Mediterranean Africa, Nazi Europe could gain self-sufficiency in phosphate. Four Mediterranean countries are producers of phosphate—their combined production in 1937 amounting to 1,314,000 metric tons, and their total exports to 1,380,000. This may be seen from the table given above, page 104. Palestine was the only other country in the group reporting any trade in the mineral. The *net* trade of these countries is shown below, in thousands of metric tons—the plus sign indicating net imports and the minus sign net exports.

	1937	1929
Algeria	− 167	− 232
French Morocco	− 535	− 556
Tunisia	− 539	− 842
Egypt	− 122	− 55
Palestine	+ 1	—
Total	−1,362	−1,685

These export surpluses compare closely with Nazi Europe's net imports of 1,367,000 metric tons in 1937, and 1,552,000 in 1929. Moreover, if additional markets were available, the Mediterranean countries would have no difficulty in producing and exporting additional quantities of phosphate rock.

F. Shortages of Other Minerals

A shortage in the domestic output of one or more of the major minerals, such as copper, lead, zinc, or petroleum, is a great handicap to any industrial country that does not have easy access to foreign sources of supply. But many other minerals are also of strategic importance in this machine age, although they may be required in relatively small amounts. In some of these, domestic production is entirely lacking in Nazi Europe, and in some it falls short of meeting consumption requirements.

More than 90 per cent of the area's consumption of manganese ore was supplied from imports in 1937. All of the big steel manufacturing countries were entirely dependent on imports for their supply of this important alloy metal, which has long been indispensable in the manufacture of practically all kinds of steel. In fact, so far as Nazi Europe was concerned, production was confined to the Balkan region (including Italy) and Sweden. The trade and production of the area are shown below, in thousands of metric tons of manganese content—the plus sign indicating net imports and the minus sign net exports.[7]

Countries	Net Trade	Production	Countries	Net Trade	Production
I. Bulgaria....	—	1	IV. Germany....	+253	—
Rumania....	− 8	15	Belgium-Luxemburg	+159	—
Yugoslavia..	—	2	Czechoslovakia....	+ 33	18
Total.....	− 8	18	France.......	+237	—
			Italy........	+ 36	12
II. Denmark...	+ 1	—	Total......	+718	30
Hungary....	− 5	10			
Netherlands.	+ 6	—	All Nazi Europe....	+824	64
Poland.....	+35	—			
Spain.......	+ 5	—			
Total.....	+42	10			
III. Greece......	− 1	4			
Norway.....	+67	—			
Sweden.....	+ 6	2			
Total.....	+72	6			

[7] Figures were compiled from publications of the Imperial Institute and from U. S. Bureau of Mines, *Foreign Minerals Quarterly*, 1938–39, and omit ores with less than 30 per cent manganese content.

Imports of manganese ore came principally from British India, Russia, and South Africa, with smaller amounts from other parts of Africa and from Brazil. The importance of Nazi Europe's trade to the principal producers of this metal in 1937 is indicated by the figures given below (in thousands of metric tons of manganese content).

Exporting Country	Exports to Nazi Europe	Total Exports	Production
British India.................	251	498	534
Russia........................	211	470	1,323
Union of South Africa.........	148	207	269
Gold Coast...................	70	278	278
Brazil.......................	38	116	122
Five countries..............	718	1,569	2,526
WORLD TOTAL[8].................	843	1,909	2,846

Production of 54,000 tons was reported by Egypt and 36,000 tons by French Morocco. Acquisition of those countries, therefore, would more than double the area's production of manganese, but would still leave it primarily dependent on imports.

Nazi Europe is deficient in many other metals required for the manufacture of alloy steels. These include cobalt, chrome ore, molybdenum, tungsten, and vanadium. Used in various combinations and proportions, such metals give to steel precisely those qualities that are required for each of a great variety of special purposes.

Cobalt, which is used in making the hardest of cutting steels, and also as a coloring agent in the ceramic industry, has been imported principally from French Morocco and the Belgian Congo. Other important sources for this metal are Northern Rhodesia, Canada,

[8] World exports to Nazi Europe include intra-area exports amounting to 13,000 tons.

and Burma. Inside the area there has been some small-scale production in Germany and Greece, and enough from Italy to warrant the prediction of an export surplus from that country in the near future.[9]

Chromite, the ore for chromium—used principally in the manufacture of stainless steel—is produced in Yugoslavia, Greece, and Bulgaria. Their aggregate production, however, has been far short of the area's consumption requirements. Turkey is one of the world's largest producers of this ore, but in the past her total output has been smaller than the import requirements of the German area. Russia's output is also large, but is all consumed by domestic industries. Other large sources of supply are Southern Rhodesia and the Union of South Africa.

Molybdenum is almost a monopoly product of the United States. Norway, with less than 3 per cent of the world's total output, ranks third among producing countries. French Morocco and Turkey produce the metal, but in very small amounts.

Nickel—used as an alloy in many kinds of steel, particularly stainless steel, and in certain grades of cast iron, as well as for nickel plating, etc.—is imported from Canada and New Caledonia. The domestic supply for the area—from Norway and Greece—falls far short of meeting requirements.

Tungsten—used for filaments in electric lamps and as the principal alloying element in high-speed steels—has been imported principally from China. It is not produced in important amounts in any German-area or Mediterranean country except Portugal which, as a rule, accounted for about 5 per cent of the world total.

Vanadium—used in the manufacture of steel for ar-

[9] U. S. Bureau of Mines, *Minerals Yearbook*, 1940, p. 614.

mor plate and for high-speed tools—has not been produced in any part of the German or Mediterranean areas and was imported by only two of them, Germany and France. Taken together, these two countries have consumed about 35 per cent of world output in past years—the principal producers of the metal being Peru and British Southwest Africa.

In normal years the area has depended upon imports for many other industrial minerals. Among these are antimony, asbestos, mica, and tin, also graphite, industrial diamonds, and quartz crystals—all highly important for modern industry.

Antimony, which must be added to lead to make the perfect type metal, has been imported principally from China. A number of the German-area and Mediterranean countries are producers of this metal, the largest of these being Yugoslavia. In normal years, however, production has fallen far short of requirements.

Asbestos of the spinning variety, which is required for the manufacture of brake linings for motor vehicles, has been imported principally from Canada, Southern Rhodesia, Russia, and the Union of South Africa. None of this variety is produced in either the European or Mediterranean areas, although there has been some production of the kind used for insulation purposes.

Mica, a mineral that is practically indispensable in the manufacture of electrical equipment for the automobile, airplane, and radio industries, has been imported from British India. None is produced in the area except small amounts of an inferior grade, in Norway.

Tin is a strategic mineral used in the manufacture of bearings for all kinds of machinery and all kinds of transportation equipment, for coating steel to make "tin" cans, for solders, bronzes, gun metals, and many other industrial purposes. Small amounts are produced in Spain and Portugal, but the bulk of the area's requirements are supplied from British Malaya, Bolivia, and the Dutch East Indies.

II. EXPORTABLE MINERALS

Nazi Europe is in a favorable position with regard to a number of highly important industrial minerals and fertilizer materials. The most important of these are iron and steel, coal, bauxite, nitrogenous fertilizers, potash, mercury, and gypsum.

A. Iron and Steel

A larger tonnage of new iron is taken from world mines and processed annually than of any other single metal or, in fact, than all of the other metals taken together. The primary importance of iron and steel to any industrial country is a matter of common knowledge.

Nazi Europe, as a rule, has had relatively small net exports of iron and steel. Cut off from outside sources, the area could have supplied its consumptive requirements for iron ore from domestic production, while smelter and steel-mill capacity was also fully adequate.[10] Practically all states in the area were producing some ore in 1937, and practically all of them had some trade in ore, scrap, and new metal. Only a few were without any smelter and steel-mill capacity.

The table on page 112 and 113, shows ore trade and production (in terms of the iron content of the ore). It also includes similar data for pig iron, and for steel ingots and castings, and trade figures for scrap iron.

---

[10] However, because of shortages in many of the alloy metals, it could not have manufactured any of the high-grade, special-purpose steels required for the manufacture of modern machines and machine tools.

Information is not available concerning the collection and use of domestic scrap in each of the several countries, but for the area as a whole this probably amounted to something like 13 million metric tons in 1937.[11]

As the table indicates, the smelting industry of the area consumed most of the output of ore—combining this with some scrap and other materials in the production of pig iron. Practically all of the pig iron produced was also kept within the area and, together with relatively large quantities of scrap and various alloy metals, was converted into steel ingots, castings, blooms, billets, bars, and slabs. Only 1 or 2 per cent of these products of the steel industry were exported. The other 98 or 99 per cent went into the finishing mills, to be manufactured into structural shapes, rails, car wheels, axles and shafts, tubes and bars, wire, armor plate, and the many other manufactured products that entered into Europe's export trade.

France was the largest producer of iron ore in the area and, in many years, the largest in the world. Her ores are of low grade, however, while those of the second largest producer, Sweden, have a very high iron content. Germany, the area's third largest producer of ore in 1937 (though ranking considerably lower in 1929) was by far the largest importer and consumer of ore, and the largest manufacturer of pig iron and steel. The greater part of these ore imports came from France, in exchange for high-grade German coal. Some came from Sweden, principally in exchange for German manufactures. In

[11] German consumption of scrap iron and steel in 1937 has been estimated at 10 million metric tons (U. S. Bureau of Mines, *Yearbook*, 1940, p. 525), of which 555,000 metric tons were imported. A year earlier, 1936, the scrap consumption of the principal European steel producers was roughly as follows: Germany 7.1 million metric tons, France 2.1 millions, Belgium 0.4 millions, Luxemburg 0.2 millions (U. S. Tariff Commission, *Iron and Steel*, Report No. 128, 2d Series, 1938, p. 62).

IRON AND STEEL TRADE

(In thousands

I. IN 1937

Countries (By groups)	Ore[b] (Estimated iron content)		Pig Iron and Ferro-alloys		Scrap Iron (Net trade)[e]	Steel Ingots and Castings	
	Net Trade[c]	Production	Net Trade[e]	Production		Net Imports[e]	Production
I. Bulgaria........:	− 10	10	+ 5	—	− 5	...	—
Rumania........	+ 27	67	+ 8	127	+ 21	+ 75	239
Yugoslavia......	− 300	364	+ 9	41	+ 26	+ 10	169
Total.........	− 283	441	+ 22	168	+ 42	+ 85	408
II. Denmark........	+ 52	—	+ 62	—	− 122		—
Hungary........	+ 195	100	+ 33	358	+ 59	− 24	665
Netherlands.....	+ 464	—	−223	299	− 473	—	—
Poland..........	+ 324	281	− 3	720	+ 642	+ 26	1,467
Portugal........	− 155	108	+ 12	—	− 24	+ 12	—
Spain[d].........	− 1,577	1,363	+ 1	130	+ 37	+ 1	168
Total........	− 697	1,852	−118	1,507	+ 119	+ 15	2,300
III. Albania.........	—	—	—	—	—	—	—
Greece.........	− 245	228	—	—	− 22	+ 8	—
Norway.........	− 953	1,190	−135	181	− 13	− 3	—
Sweden.........	− 8,810	9,205	+ 73	693	+ 86	− 26	1,106
Total........	−10,008	10,623	− 62	874	+ 51	− 21	1,106
IV. Germany........	+11,118	2,929	+ 65	15,960	+ 555	− 44	19,356
Austria.........	− 100	672	− 22	388	+ 56	− 59	657
Belgium-Luxemburg....	+ 3,970	2,360	+259	6,316	− 219	−426	6,373
Czechoslovakia...	+ 875	607	+ 30	1,675	+ 250	− 10	2,315
France..........	− 6,174	11,578	−402	7,916	− 122	−263	7,920
Italy..	+ 30	896	+ 20	874	+ 545	+ 40	2,099
Switzerland......	− 65	40	+170[e]	—	− 95	...[e]	—
Total........	+ 9,654	19,082	+120	33,129	+ 970	−762	38,720
All Nazi Europe......	− 1,334	31,998	− 38	35,678	+1,182	−683	42,534

[a] Compiled from League of Nations, *Statistical Year-book*, 1938–39 and 1939–40, and *International Trade in Certain Raw Materials and Foodstuffs*, 1938; from official trade reports; and from Imperial Institute, *The Mineral Industry of the British Empire and Foreign Countries, Statistical Summary*, 1929–1934 and 1936–1938.
[b] Includes the estimated iron content of pyrites (figures in thousands of metric tons): in production, 2,324 in 1937 and 2,396 in 1929; net exports, 310 in 1937 and 223 in 1929. Not all of the iron in pyrites was used in the production of pig iron.

an effort to avoid a deficiency in imports, Germany turned to her low-grade, non-commercial, domestic deposits—a project that was not organized until the middle of 1937, with initial production expected in 1940. France was second as a producer and consumer of pig iron and steel, and the Belgium-Luxemburg Union ranked third.

AND PRODUCTION, 1937, 1929[a]

of metric tons)

II. IN 1929

Countries (By groups)	Ore (Estimated iron content)		Pig Iron and Ferro-alloys		Scrap Iron (Net trade)[c]	Steel Ingots and Castings	
	Net Trade[c]	Production	Net Trade[c]	Production		Net Trade[c]	Production
I. Bulgaria........	—	—	+ 5	—	—[f]	...	—
Rumania........	—	50	+ 8[f]	72		+ 7[f]	161
Yugoslavia......	− 227	260	+ 12	31	+ 24	+ 8	97
Total........	− 227	310	+ 25	103	+ 24	+ 15	258
II. Denmark........	+ 29	—	+ 54	—	− 75	—	—
Hungary........	+ 30	87	+ 40	368	+ 10	+ 1	514
Netherlands.....	+ 286	—	−148	260	− 248	− 12	—
Poland..........	+ 292	189	+ 3	706	+ 514	+ 37	1,377
Portugal........	− 121	121	—	—	...[g]	+ 7[g]	—
Spain..........	− 3,716	4,603	+ 17	753	+ 216	+ 6	1,003
Total........	− 3,200	5,000	− 34	2,087	+ 417	+ 39	2,894
III. Albania........	—	—	—	—	—	—	—
Greece.........	− 104	176	+ 3	—	− 5	—	—
Norway.........	− 694	736	−115	153	− 37	—	4
Sweden.........	− 6,536	6,981	− 10	524	+ 17	− 5	694
Total........	− 7,334	7,893	−122	677	− 25	− 5	698
IV. Germany........	+ 9,250	2,221	−279	13,239	+ 120	− 333	16,023
Austria..........	− 53	597	− 14	459	− 16	− 3	644
Belgium-Luxemburg....	+ 5,040	2,357	+553	6,947	− 165	− 320	6,812
Czechoslovakia...	+ 851	600	+ 30	1,645	+ 278	− 50	2,193
France..........	− 5,077	18,081	−517	12,467	− 279	− 449	11,926
Italy...........	+ 48	626	+174	727	+ 995	+ 40	2,122
Switzerland......	− 17	—	+170	—	− 86	...[e]	—
Total........	+10,042	24,482	+117[e]	35,484	+ 847	−1,115	39,720
All Nazi Europe......	− 719	37,685	− 14	38,351	+1,263	−1,066	43,570

[c] Net imports (+), net exports (−). In the case of steel ingots and castings, the trade figures exclude tool and other special steels but include blooms, billets, and slabs. Owing to differences in tariff classifications the statistics are not strictly comparable from country to country.

[d] Trade data for Spain in 1937 are estimates based on statistics of countries trading with Spain.

[e] For Switzerland, trade in pig iron, etc., includes trade in steel ingots.

[f] Trade data for Rumania are for 1930 since statistics for 1929 were not available.

[g] For Portugal, trade in scrap is included with trade in steel ingots, etc.

A very large proportion of the trade in ore and pig iron was intra-area in character, but crude steel was shipped to many outside markets. Total ore imports in 1937, in terms of iron content, amounted to roughly 17.4 million metric tons. Of this amount only 2.3 million tons came from outside sources, including 1.5 millions from Spanish Morocco and French North Africa. Intra-area iron ore imports thus amounted to 15.1 millions out of the 17.4 million total. On the other hand, less than one-third of the relatively small total (975,000 tons) of crude steel exports went to other countries inside the area.

The inclusion of the Mediterranean area would not change Nazi Europe's position in iron and steel, except in the case of ore. However, it would considerably increase the exportable supply of ore. Four countries of Mediterranean Africa reported net exports—aggregating 2.6 million metric tons in 1937 and 2.1 millions in 1929. No trade in iron ore was reported from Mediterranean Asia in 1937, and only 1,000 (from Turkey) in 1929.

The ore trade of these countries is shown below, in thousands of metric tons of iron content, the minus sign indicating net exports.

	1937		1929	
All Nazi Europe..........		−1,334		− 719
Mediterranean Africa:				
Algeria................	−1,354		−1,070	
French Morocco........	− 14		—	
Tunisia................	− 496		− 500	
Spanish Morocco.......	− 763	−2,627	− 575	−2,145
Turkey...................		—		− 1
Total................		−3,961		−2,865

Scrap iron net exports from the Mediterranean area amounted to only 70,000 tons in 1937 compared with net imports into Nazi Europe of 1,182,000 tons. Comparable figures for 1929 were 55,000 and 1,263,000, respectively.[12]

Pig iron and crude steel have been imported into

[12] In 1937, trade in scrap was reported by seven countries, the largest being net exports of 44,000 from French Morocco. In 1929, Egypt (with net exports of 26,000) was the largest of the five Mediterranean traders in scrap.

some of the Mediterranean countries, but in relatively small amounts. Net imports of pig iron amounted to 4,000 tons (for two countries) in 1937, and to 6,000 (for three countries) in 1929. Net imports of crude steel aggregated 22,000 tons (for four countries) in 1937, Turkey alone accounting for 17,000 tons. In 1929 net imports of crude steel (into two countries) amounted to 17,000 tons, of which 16,000 were taken by the French colony of Tunisia.

By acquiring control over the Mediterranean area, therefore, Nazi Europe would increase its existing capacity to produce an exportable supply of ore or metal. However, Europe's problem with regard to iron and steel has been principally a problem of markets, and the domestic market for pig iron and crude steel would be practically unchanged by the inclusion of the Mediterranean group of countries.

B. Coal

Coal is used principally as a source of power and heat, and in the production of coke, gas, and a considerable number of by-products. It has long been of basic importance in the metallurgical industries—in the smelting of ores, in the refining process, and in converting the metals into partly finished and finished goods. At the present time it is also being used—in Germany, for the most part—as a raw material for the production of benzol and synthetic gasoline.

In the past Nazi Europe has imported some of the coal consumed in the area. In 1929, net imports accounted for 9 per cent of total consumption, reduced to 4 per cent in 1937. Figures showing the area's trade and production are given on page 116.

COAL TRADE AND PRODUCTION, 1937, 1929[a]

(In thousands of metric tons)

Countries (By groups)	1937[b]		1929	
	Net Trade[c]	Production	Net Trade[c]	Production
I. Bulgaria	+ 1	698	+ 1	605
Rumania	+ 93	929	+ 257[d]	1,263
Yugoslavia	+ 452	1,952	+ 677	2,157
Total	+ 546	3,579	+ 935	4,025
II. Denmark	+ 6,278	—	+ 5,697	341
Hungary	+ 551	3,602	+ 1,818	3,174
Netherlands	− 1,268	14,368	+ 4,167	11,633
Poland	−11,291	36,222	−13,730	46,254
Portugal	+ 1,367	257	+ 1,144	207
Spain	+ 1,177	7,169	+ 2,092	7,328
Total	− 3,186	61,618	+ 1,188	68,937
III. Albania	—	3	—	1
Greece	+ 993	65	+ 810	78
Norway	+ 2,735	780[e]	+ 2,798	251
Sweden	+ 9,719	460	+ 6,689	395
Total	+13,447	1,308	+10,297	725
IV. Germany	−45,733	230,690	−32,970	207,255
Austria	+ 3,450	1,851	+ 6,482	1,970
Belgium-Luxemburg	+ 4,234	29,859	+11,233	26,940
Czechoslovakia	− 2,734	27,564	− 1,255	27,815
France	+29,623	44,657	+27,493	67,758
Italy	+12,933	1,229	+14,767	418
Switzerland	+ 3,509	—	+ 3,529	509
Total	+ 5,282	335,850	+29,279	332,665
All Nazi Europe	+16,089	402,355	+41,699	406,352

[a] Production includes lignite and brown coal, and trade includes lignite and brown coal, coke, and brickettes, all converted to coal equivalents. Bunker coal (reported as 6,014,000 tons in the export statistics for 1937, and 5,732,000 for 1929) is not included in the computation of net trade. The data are compiled from official trade reports; from League of Nations, *Statistical Yearbook*, 1938–1939 and 1939–1940; and from Imperial Institute, *The Mineral Industry of the British Empire and Foreign Countries, Statistical Summary*, 1929–31, and 1936–38.

[b] Figures for Spain are for 1935, the latest available.

[c] Net imports (+), net exports (−).

[d] Since the export figure for 1929 was not available, that for 1930 was used.

[e] All from Spitzbergen.

By far the larger part of the coal trade was intra-area in character. Germany and Poland were the principal exporters, both of them selling principally within the area. The Netherlands was a net importer in its trade with outside countries—buying principally from the United Kingdom—but was a net exporter in its trade with other German-area countries. A comparison of the intra-area and external trade in coal is summarized in the accompanying table.

WHERE NAZI EUROPE BOUGHT AND SOLD COAL, 1937[a]
(Figures are in thousands of metric tons)

Group	Exports to and Imports from Inside the Area			Exports to and Imports from Outside Countries		
	Exports	Imports	Net	Exports	Imports	Net
I..........	3	504	+ 501	34	79	+ 45
II..........	15,929	7,989	−7,940	3,287	6,858	+ 3,571
III..........	—	7,651	+7,651	484	6,280	+ 5,796
IV..........	51,558	51,346	− 212	11,785	17,279	+ 5,494
Total........	67,490	67,490	0	15,590	30,496	+14,906

[a] Data are from sources cited in footnote *a*, p. 116. Spain is not included here since 1937 figures were not available.

Cross-channel trade with Great Britain supplied practically all the coal brought in from outside sources. Denmark, Norway, Sweden, and Italy were large importers from Britain, and even Germany bought some British coal. However, Britain's advantages in the trade with these countries resulted from economies in transportation, rather than any deficiency in the area's capacity to produce coal.

The Mediterranean area, like Nazi Europe, has been on an import basis for coal. Only one of the Mediterranean countries, Turkey, has developed an exportable surplus of coal. The figures which follow show the net imports of these countries, in thousands of metric tons (with the minus sign indicating net exports).

Territory	1937		1929	
Nazi Europe....................		16,089		41,699
Mediterranean Africa:				
Algeria.......................	625		767	
French Morocco..............	81		182	
Tunisia.......................	255		253	
Egypt........................	1,349		1,245	
Libya........................	44		...	
Spanish Morocco..............	7	2,361	...	2,447
Mediterranean Asia:				
Turkey[13].....................	−257		− 8	
Syria and Lebanon.............	128		38	
Palestine.....................	96		29	
Cyprus.......................	5	− 28	12	71
Total..........................		18,422		44,217

Coal for these Mediterranean countries undoubtedly could have been produced from German and Polish mines. The problem involved was transportation costs. But with cheaper coal from Britain cut off, and with transportation costs disregarded, the output of coal from principal producing countries in Nazi Europe probably would expand to meet the needs of the larger area.

C. Bauxite and Aluminum

Bauxite is the principal ore from which aluminum is produced. Other minerals, such as alunite, leucite, and nepheline, also contain the metal, but for many years to come production is likely to be limited almost entirely to bauxite because of its higher metal content and plentiful supply. Something like one-third to one-half of the annual supply of bauxite is used in the production of aluminum. The rest is used in the manufacture of aluminous cement, refractories, abrasives, etc. Aluminum is used in the manufacture of electrical

[13] The 1929 figure for Turkey is a rough estimate.

conductors and appliances, and in many other familiar ways.

Nazi Europe has been practically self-sufficient in bauxite, and has exported small quantities of aluminum. Taken as a whole, it accounts for about 55 per cent of the world's bauxite production, and for almost 50 per cent

BAUXITE AND ALUMINUM TRADE AND PRODUCTION, 1937, 1929[a]

[In thousands of metric tons; net imports (+), net exports (−)]

Countries (By groups)	Bauxite				Aluminum			
	1937[b]		1929		1937[b]		1929	
	Net Trade	Pro-duction	Net Trade	Pro-duction	Net Trade	Pro-duction	Net Trade	Pro-duction
I. Bulgaria......	—	—	—	—	+ .1	—	—	—
Rumania.....	—	—	—	1	+ .2	—	—	—
Yugoslavia...	− 388	358	− 67	104	− .1	.2	—	—
Total......	− 388	358	− 67	105	+ .2	.2	—	—
II. Denmark.....	—	—	—	—	+ .9	—	+ .1	—
Hungary.....	− 480	452	−101	389	+ .4	1.2	+ .5	—
Netherlands..	—	—	—	—	+ 1.9	—	+ .8	—
Poland.......	+ 4	—	—	—	+ 1.2	—	+ .7	—
Portugal.....	—	—	—	—	—	—	+ .1	—
Spain........	+ 8	—	+ 6	1	—	1.3	− .2	1.0
Total......	− 468	452	− 95	390	+ 4.4	2.5	+ 2.0	1.0
III. Albania......	—	—	—	—				
Greece.......	− 122	147	—	6	—	—	—	—
Norway......	+ 115	—	+121	—	−21.5	23.0	−29.6	29.1
Sweden......	+ 20	—	+ 13	—	+ 2.9	1.8	+ 1.6	—
Total......	+ 13	147	+134	6	−18.6	24.8	−28.0	29.1
IV. Germany.....	+1,307	20	+382	7	+ 5.8	127.6	+10.1	33.3
Austria......	—	3	—	—	− 3.2	4.4	− 3.2	2.7
Belgium-Luxemburg.	+ 2	—	+ 2	—	+ 3.4	—	+ 2.0	—
Czechoslovakia	—	—	—	—	+ 4.8	—	—	—
France.......	− 356	691	−308	666	− 6.8	34.5	− 2.0	29.1
Italy........	− 164	387	− 75	193	+ 3.5	22.9	+ 2.3	7.0
Switzerland...	+ 5	—	+ 83	—	−14.9	25.0	−14.9	20.7
Total......	+ 794	1,101	+ 84	866	− 7.4	214.4	− 5.7	92.8
All Nazi Europe...	− 49	2,058	+ 56	1,367	−21.4	241.9	−31.7	122.9

[a] Trade figures for bauxite include alumina in terms of bauxite. For aluminum, the trade figures include ingots and other crude shapes and scrap. Compiled from official trade reports and from Imperial Institute, *The Mineral Industry of the British Empire and Foreign Countries, Statistical Summary*, 1929–1931 and 1936–1938.
[b] Figures for Spain are for 1935; 1937 not available.

of the world's aluminum output. Its principal bauxite producers are France, Hungary, Italy, and Yugoslavia. In aluminum, the one outstanding producer is Germany. Figures covering the trade and production in the ore and metal are given in the table above.

Germany's dominating position in the aluminum in dustry has been based on imports from other parts of the area, and on efficient utilization of her low-grade coal resources for providing the power required for aluminum production.[14] The four other principal European producers of aluminum—France, Italy, Norway, and Switzerland—are alike in having cheap hydro-electric power. But while the first two of these countries utilize ores produced at home, the other two import the bauxite and alumina they consume.

Practically all of the bauxite trade has been intra-area in character. Trade in this ore was considerably larger in 1937 than in 1929, the greater part of the increase representing a larger movement of ore to Germany from Yugoslavia, Hungary, and France. The small amounts of bauxite imported from outside countries came principally from the United States in 1929, and from the Dutch East Indies in 1937.

In aluminum, the relatively small trade has been divided almost equally between intra-area and external trade. In the main, as the table on page 119 shows, the greater part of the aluminum production was for domestic consumption. Within the area, the producing countries were also net importers of aluminum. In the trade with outside countries, more than half of the total imports came from Canada, the United States, and the United Kingdom, while more than half of the exports went to the United States and the United Kingdom.

No trade in bauxite, and practically none in aluminum, is reported for *any* part of Mediterranean Africa or Asia.

---

[14] Two principal steps are involved in the manufacture of aluminum: extraction of alumina from bauxite; reduction of alumina to aluminum. All countries except Germany use water-generated power for the second process.

D. Nitrate

Nitrogen in the soil is one of the three elements absolutely essential for plant life. And since old soils are likely to be deficient in this plant food, use of nitrogenous fertilizers is of special importance in Europe. Until Germany began commercial production of synthetic or artificial nitrogen, shortly before the World War, practically all of the world's supply came from Chile's large natural deposits. After the war, the cost of producing artificial nitrates was gradually reduced in Europe and the United States until it was lower than the delivered cost of the Chilean product. At the present time Chile accounts for less than 10 per cent of the world's supply. Well over 60 per cent is derived by the synthetic method, and the rest is a by-product obtained principally from the coking of coals. About 85 to 90 per cent of the world's consumption of nitrogen compounds is in the form of fertilizers. In wartime the second largest use is for the manufacture of ammunition; in peacetime, for industrial explosives.

In 1929 Nazi Europe's consumption of nitrates slightly exceeded production, but in 1937 the area was on an export basis. The shift from an import to an export basis for the area as a whole resulted from changes under way in many of the individual countries, and not, as one might perhaps suppose, from an increase in German production. A rough indication of the changes taking place in the several countries, as well as in the area as a whole, is given by the accompanying table, page 122.

Production data for the Netherlands, Norway, Belgium-Luxemburg, France, and Italy all show substantial increases, while the trade figures for the area show that eight countries were net exporters in 1937 as compared with four in 1929. In Germany, however, there was a

NITROGENOUS FERTILIZER TRADE AND PRODUCTION, 1937, 1929[a]

(In thousands of metric tons of nitrogen content)

Countries (By groups)	1937[b]		1929	
	Net Imports (+) Net Exports (−)	Production	Net Imports (+) Net Exports (−)	Production
I. Bulgaria	+ .1	—	+ .1	—
Rumania	+ .2	—	− 3.5	3.7
Yugoslavia	− 6.9	8.9	− 6.0	9.0
Total	− 6.6	8.9	− 9.4	12.7
II. Denmark	+ 31.9	—	+ 47.8	.8
Hungary	− 5.6[c]	.3	+ 2.9	.3
Netherlands	− 22.5	70.5	+ 87.1	12.2
Poland	− 13.4	43.6	+ 14.4	49.6
Portugal	+ 15.0	—	+ 3.7	—
Spain	+122.9	2.6	+ 83.2	5.3
Total	+128.3	117.0	+239.1	68.2
III. Albania	—	—	—	—
Greece	+ 4.3[d]	—	+ 2.6	—
Norway	− 70.8	87.9	− 52.2[c]	48.2
Sweden	+ 18.5	6.6	+ 13.5	6.7
Total	− 48.0	94.5	− 36.1	54.9
IV. Germany	−164.7	700.0	−308.1	800.4
Austria	+ 4.9	1.3[d]	+ 4.6	1.2
Belgium-Luxemburg	− 33.5	69.1	+ 31.4	39.8
Czechoslovakia	+ 1.1	22.9	+ 17.6	23.0
France	+ 23.4	164.7	+122.4	80.3
Italy	+ 55.8	102.2	+ 25.3	50.3
Switzerland	− 2.7	2.9	+ .1	2.2
Total	−115.7	1,063.1	−106.7	997.2
All Nazi Europe	− 42.0	1,283.5	+ 86.9	1,133.0

[a] Production includes some nitrogen for other than fertilizer uses. Compiled from International Institute of Agriculture, *International Yearbook of Agricultural Statistics*, 1931–32 and 1938–39, and from Imperial Institute, *The Mineral Industry of the British Empire and Foreign Countries, Statistical Summary*, 1929–1931 and 1936–1938.

[b] Figures for Spain are for 1935; 1937 data are not available.

[c] This may mean that the basic data are incomplete, or that exports were made from stocks.

[d] 1936 figure; 1937 data not available.

considerable decline in reported production, and also a decline in net exports—but an increase in consumption.

For the area as a whole, the production of nitrate for fertilizers increased from 1.13 million metric tons (nitrogen content) in 1929 to 1.28 millions in 1937. This compares with a rise in world production from 1.93 millions to about 2.50 millions.[15] For the future it would seem that the area may expect to be more than self-sufficient, for large additions to plant capacity undoubtedly have been made since 1937. However, there seems little prospect of any great increase in the export trade in this commodity, because large increases in plant capacity are also being made in many other parts of the world.

The Mediterranean countries have been on an import basis for nitrate. The principal consumer among these countries has been Egypt, accounting for net imports of 118,800 metric tons out of a total of 123,600 in 1937, and 53,500 out of 55,800 in 1929. Thus net exports of nitrate would be somewhat smaller for the larger area than for Nazi Europe alone.

E. Potash

Production of potash, another essential fertilizer material, was practically a German monopoly until conditions during the first World War sent the price of the mineral soaring. This led to an intensive search for potash in many countries, with important deposits discovered in the United States and Soviet Russia, and smaller ones elsewhere. As a result, Germany's share of world production was reduced from 95 per cent in 1918 to 61 per cent in 1937. Roughly 93 per cent of world output is used for fertilizer purposes. The rest is used

[15] Of the total world production, Chile accounted for about 518,300 metric tons in 1929, and 208,900 in 1937.

in the manufacture of soap, high-grade glass, and matches, and in minor quantities in the manufacture of explosives, in the tanning and dyeing industries, in metallurgy, and in various other industries.

Exports to outside markets amounted to 21 per cent of the area's potash production in 1929, increased to 24 per cent in 1937. The product of the whole area was accounted for by three countries in 1937: Germany, France, and Poland. Spain was also a producer in 1935, but by 1937 the civil war had brought an end to that country's output, and its markets had been taken over by other European producers. The accompanying table, page 125, gives trade and production data for the several countries of the area, and for all of them combined.

Taken as a whole, the area produced practically all of the world's supply of potash in 1929—that is, it produced 2,061,000 metric tons, K_2O content, out of a total of 2,123,000 tons. By 1937, outside areas had increased their production, so that Nazi Europe now accounted for 2,279,000 metric tons as compared with 2,787,000 for all countries. However, the area's net exports to outside countries were considerably higher in 1937 than they had been in 1929. Consumption of this mineral in outside countries was increasing at a faster rate than in Nazi Europe.

Potash exports went principally to the United States. Japan was the market of second importance in 1937 and the British Isles third. Very small amounts were taken in other outside markets. Shipments from one part of Nazi Europe to another accounted for more than 40 per cent of the potash exports of the area, or for more than the imports into any other large world area. The accompanying table shows the principal outside markets for potash, comparing their imports from Nazi Europe

POTASH TRADE AND PRODUCTION, 1937, 1929[a]
(In thousands of metric tons of K_2O content)

Countries (By groups)	1937 Net Imports[b]	1937 Production	1929 Net Imports[b]	1929 Production
I. Bulgaria...............	—	—	—	—
Rumania...............	—	—	—	—
Yugoslavia.............	1	—	—	—
Total...............	1	—	—	—
II. Denmark..............	37	—	18	—
Hungary...............	1	—	1	—
Netherlands............	101	—	118	—
Poland................	— 23	100	23	62
Portugal...............	2	—	—	—
Spain.................	c	c	— 3	24
Total...............	118	100	157	86
III. Albania...............	—	—	—	—
Greece................	3	—	4	—
Norway...............	12	—	5	—
Sweden...............	34	—	37	—
Total...............	49	—	46	—
IV. Germany...............	−650	1,690	−475	1,483
Austria................	6	—	5	—
Belgium-Luxemburg......	17	—	49	—
Czechoslovakia..........	33	—	26	—
France................	−149	489	−267	492
Italy.................	13	—	17	—
Switzerland............	9	—	7	—
Total...............	−721	2,179	−638	1,975
All Nazi Europe............	−553	2,279	−435	2,061

[a] Trade figures for 1937 are based on export data of the exporting countries —Germany, France, Belgium-Luxemburg, Poland, and Spain—since export data are given in greater detail than import. Trade figures for 1929 were compiled from U. S. Bureau of Mines, *Potash*, Economic Paper 16. Production data were compiled from International Institute of Agriculture, *International Yearbook of Agricultural Statistics*, 1931–32 and 1938–39.

Trade data are only for those salts which are primarily used as fertilizers (kainite, carnallite, and sylvite; potassium chloride; potassium sulphate; potassium-magnesium sulphate; potassium nitrate). Production, which is reported on a mine basis, includes all K_2O available for consumption, including that not used by the fertilizer industry.

[b] Net exports (−).

[c] In 1935 Spain produced 121,000 tons K_2O content, which was apparently all exported; no later data are available.

with their imports from all sources and their domestic production.

PRINCIPAL OUTSIDE MARKETS FOR POTASH, 1937, 1929[a]
(Amounts are in thousands of metric tons of K_2O content)

Importing Areas	1937			1929		
	Imports from Nazi Europe	Total Imports	Production	Imports from Nazi Europe	Total Imports	Production
Western Hemisphere:						
United States.......	267	275	258	276	276	56
Canada.............	16	22	—	7	9	—
Two countries.....	283	297	258	283	285	56
Australasia:						
Japan..............	120	128	4[b]	35	41	1
New Zealand.......	5	5	--	1	3	—
Australia...........	4	10	—	9	2	—
India and Ceylon....	3	6	9	10	10	5
Four areas........	132	149	13	55	56	6
British Isles..........	77	79	—	62	68	—
Baltic states[c].........	28	28	—	13	13	—
Total for markets listed.	520	553	271	413	422	62
WORLD TOTAL[d]........	955	986	2,787	776	785	2,123

[a] Compiled from sources cited in footnote *a* to table on p. 125.

[b] Production in 1936; figure for 1937 not available.

[c] Finland, Estonia, Latvia, and Lithuania.

[d] Total imports include the intra-area trade of Nazi Europe, amounting to 397,000 metric tons in 1937 and 341,000 tons in 1929.

Nazi Europe's position with regard to potash would not be substantially changed by the inclusion of Mediterranean Asia and Africa. The combined trade of these countries in 1937 showed net exports of 9,000 metric tons—Palestine reporting net exports of 15,000, and the three North African colonies offsetting this with net imports of 6,000. In 1929 only Algeria and French Morocco participated in the trade, their combined net imports amounting to 7,000 tons.

F. Other Exportable Minerals

In the past the German area has produced exportable supplies of a few other minerals. Among these were gypsum, mercury, and sulphur.

Gypsum, which is used in the manufacture of portland cement, in plaster of paris, and in wall plaster, insulation materials, and other supplies for the building trades, is produced in many parts of the area. Practically all of the world's supply of the translucent variety known as alabaster comes from the Italian province of Pisa.

Mercury, which is used in the drug and chemical industries, in the manufacture of high explosives, of paint for ship bottoms, and in various other industries, is practically a monopoly of two German-area countries, Spain and Italy.

Sulphur, which is consumed in the fertilizer, chemical, metallurgical, steel, and various other industries, is produced in Italy, in quantities more than sufficient for the needs of the whole area, while smaller amounts are also supplied from Spain.

SUMMARY

Germany's position with regard to mineral raw materials has not been improved by her acquisition of additional territory in Europe. On the contrary, Nazi Europe's net imports of industrial minerals in the past have exceeded those for Germany alone. In copper, lead, zinc, petroleum, phosphates, and manganese, net imports into the larger area have been considerably in excess of those into the old Reich. In nitrogen and potash, the exportable surplus has been smaller, while in coal a large tonnage of net exports from Germany compares with net imports into the larger area. In only two minerals has the trade position been improved. These are bauxite and aluminum, and iron and low-grade steel. These comparisons are shown in the accompanying chart.

Net Trade in Principal Industrial Minerals, 1937[a]
Germany and Nazi Europe Compared

I. METALS AND FERTILIZERS

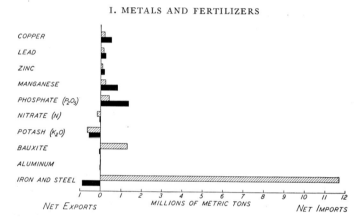

II. FUEL MINERALS

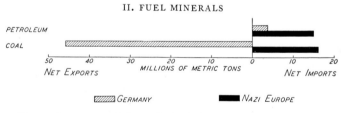

[a] Figures for copper exclude ore; for lead, zinc, and iron, include ore (metal content); and for manganese are for the ore (metal content) alone. Petroleum includes both crude and refined.

In addition to the shortages indicated by the chart, Nazi Europe like Germany is lacking in many minerals that enter world trade in small amounts but are of vital importance to modern industry. Without these minerals the area cannot make the alloy steels required in the manufacture of modern machines and machine tools, cannot make good type metal for its printing industry, has none of the bearing metals required for machines with movable parts, and is unable to make certain parts essential for the radio and for the electrical equipment of automotive machines of all kinds.

Moreover, there is such a large gap between Nazi Europe's production and consumption requirements,[16] in the case of most of the minerals imported, that there is little if any prospect of its being closed. The one important exception is coal. In 1937 the area produced more than 96 per cent of the tonnage consumed, and undoubtedly could have expanded production to cover the 4 per cent shortage in supply. However, the close balance existing between the output and use of coal, in the area as a whole, does raise questions concerning the amounts available for use in the manufacture of gasoline and other synthetic products.

Western Hemisphere countries supplied more than half of the copper imported into the area, 65 per cent of the lead, 53 per cent of the zinc, 60 per cent of the petroleum, and 14 per cent of the phosphates; and also afforded the principal market for the area's exports of potash. About 70 per cent of the phosphate imports came from French North Africa; most of the manganese came from British India, Russia, and the Union of South Africa; and most of the coal imports came from Great Britain.

---

[16] In most cases this gap is wide whether measured in metric tons or as percentages of consumption requirements.

CHAPTER V

HOW TRADE DEFICITS WERE MET

The analysis of preceding chapters has been confined solely to a consideration of the commodity trade. It has shown that, in the aggregate, imports have exceeded exports, but nothing has been said about the way in which funds were provided for meeting payments on these net imports. In the present chapter, therefore, the discussion will be broadened to include other types of trade and financial transactions that, taken as a whole, have provided the German-controlled area with the funds required to meet the deficits in the commodity trade. This will be followed by a consideration of the controls that Germany imposed on her foreign trade in the 1930's in order to maintain necessary imports at as high levels as possible with the reduced means of payment at her command.

I. NAZI EUROPE'S BALANCE OF PAYMENTS, 1937, 1929

Commodity trade is by far the most important of all the transactions involving the payment of foreign exchange from one country to another. In addition, however, there is the trade in shipping services, the tourist trade, the movement of funds in connection with population migrations, payments and receipts for commissions and insurance, and on interest and dividend account. Finally, there are the various classes of capital transactions concerned with borrowing, lending, and repayment operations, and with the international movement of funds for "direct" investment purposes. In the past, the trade and service accounts of each of the countries in the German-controlled area have included payments and receipts for all or most of the various classes of transactions enumerated.

For all of Nazi Europe, payments exceeded receipts in the international accounts of 1929, but a close balance was shown for 1937. New loans from outside the area helped finance the larger volume of goods imported in 1929. In 1937, however, borrowing from abroad was no longer feasible. In fact, some capital was moving out of the area. In both years, as previous chapters have already shown, there was a large excess of imports over exports in the commodity trade of the area.

The accompanying table, page 133, presents estimates with regard to the trade and service transactions of 16 German-area countries in 1929 and of 15 in 1937 (with 1936 figures substituted in a few cases where 1937 data were not available). Estimates are not readily available for either year for the other 4 countries—Albania, Portugal, Rumania,[1] and Spain.

For some of the countries, colonial territories lying outside the continent of Europe are included in the figures. The only estimates available for France cover French Indo-China and other French colonies as well as the metropolitan area. Those given for Belgium include the Belgian Congo. And for Italy, the figures we have chosen to give for 1937 include the African colonies as well as the Kingdom. It will be seen, therefore, that the area covered by the table does not coincide exactly with that of "Nazi Europe," strictly speaking.

For France and Belgium, whose colonies yield some income on investments placed there, it would be desirable for our purposes to have data for the metro-

---

[1] An incomplete statement for Rumania is available for 1929 in Virgile Madgearu, *Le Controle des Changes en Roumanie* (Bergen Conference, 1939).

politan areas alone. For Italy, however, a better picture
of the international financial situation is obtained from
empire figures than from those which treat the Kingdom
and African colonies as separate entities.

Prior to 1935, this distinction would have made little
difference in the figures for Italy. In 1935 and later
years, however, when the Italian government was send-
ing soldiers and colonists to North Africa and was furnishing them with supplies and with money payments,
figures for the Kingdom alone give a more favorable
view of the situation than actually existed. They show
such shipments of provisions as bona fide commodity exports from Italy, and the remittances sent back to
Italy by these soldiers and colonists as bona fide emigrant remittances. But they fail to point out that these
transactions were financed through the very large expenditures of the Italian government. Theoretically, the
labor of the colonists and the exploits of the soldiers
provided the Kingdom with "new investments abroad"
in exchange for such expenditures. Actually, however,
these "new investments" were largely of a political
character, promising continued outlays in the future,
rather than interest and dividend returns.

In a general way, the table indicates the sources from
which foreign exchange was obtained and the uses to
which it was put. The first column shows the net trade
in commodities—for the several countries, and for the
area as a whole.[2] The last column shows the net results

[2] It may be noted that these figures differ somewhat from those given in
the official trade reports for several of the countries. This is because (1) the
original compilers of these balance of payment estimates have included small
correction estimates for the wrong valuations known to exist in some of the
official trade figures, and have included estimates for unrecorded categories
of trade. (2) As pointed out above, available balance of payments estimates
for Belgium, France, and Italy include estimates for colonial territories lying
outside the continent of Europe.

INTERNATIONAL TRADE AND SERVICE TRANSACTIONS, 1937, 1929[a]

(In millions of dollars)

I. IN 1937

Country	Commodity Exports (+) Imports (−)	Interest and Dividend Receipts (+) Payments (−)	Receipts from Other Services (+) Payments (−)	Gold Exports (+) Imports (−)	Total Receipts (+) Payments (−)
I. Bulgaria (1936).....	+ 12.8	− 2.6	+ 1.2	—	+ 11.4
Yugoslavia (1936)...	+ 8.5	− 19.8	+ 14.3	− .2	+ 2.8
II. Denmark...........	− 21.1	− 17.7	+ 63.1	—	+ 24.3
Hungary (1936).....	+ 19.9	− 7.5	+ 7.0	—	+ 19.4
Netherlands........	− 220.0	+ 88.9	+ 152.5	−410.6	−389.2
Poland.............	− 15.5	− 33.8	+ 33.0	− 23.1	− 39.4
III. Greece............	− 63.4	—	+ 35.7	—	− 27.7
Norway............	− 100.5	− 16.2	+ 143.1	+ 7.7	+ 34.1
Sweden............	− 32.0	+ 25.8	+ 51.7	—	+ 45.5
IV. Germany...........	+ 178.1	−172.9	+ 266.1	+ 2.4	+273.7
Austria............	− 44.6	− 6.0	+ 60.3	+ 1.2	+ 10.9
Belgium-Luxemburg and Congo (1936).	− 8.8	+ 42.5	+ 68.5	+ 2.4	+104.6
Czechoslovakia......	+ 34.9	− 18.0	− 2.7	− 2.2	+ 12.0
France and colonies..	− 669.6	+261.4	+ 141.8	+433.0	+166.6
Italy and colonies...	− 366.4	− 21.0	+ 184.1	+ .6	−202.7
Total, 15 countries.	−1,287.7	+103.1	+1,219.7	+ 11.2	+ 46.3

II. IN 1929

Country	Commodity Exports (+) Imports (−)	Interest and Dividend Receipts (+) Payments (−)	Receipts from Other Services (+) Payments (−)	Gold Exports (+) Imports (−)	Total Receipts (+) Payments (−)
I. Bulgaria.............	− 12.8	− 7.8	− .5	− .2	− 21.3
Yugoslavia.........	− 9.4	− 22.3	+ 44.5	− .1	+ 12.7
II. Denmark...........	− 22.0	− 16.9	+ 48.0	—	+ 9.1
Hungary...........	− 7.7	− 28.4	− 1.0	− .8	− 37.9
Netherlands........	− 306.3	+128.0	+ 140.9	+ 10.5	− 26.9
Poland.............	− 51.9	− 42.6	+ 36.0	− 9.1	− 67.6
III. Greece.............	− 81.2	+ 7.4	+ 29.2	—	− 44.6
Norway............	− 62.2	− 18.5	+ 71.6	—	− 9.1
Sweden............	+ 9.9	+ 8.1	+ 56.2	− 2.9	+ 71.3
IV. Germany...........	+ 7.4	−190.6	− 388.3	+ 89.6	−481.9
Austria............	− 150.7	− 16.4	+ 55.9	− 3.3	−114.5
Belgium-Luxemburg and Congo.......	− 83.9	+ 53.0	+ 134.2	—	+103.3
Czechoslovakia.....	+ 15.4	− 10.7	+ 21.4	− 3.7	+ 22.4
France and colonies..	− 435.2	+113.4	+ 638.6	−336.5	− 19.7
Kingdom of Italy...	− 338.5	− 52.6	+ 306.3	− 12.1	− 96.9
Total, 15 countries.	−1,529.1	− 96.9	+1,193.0	−268.6	−701.6
Switzerland.........	− 114.7	+ 77.1	+ 26.2	+ 5.8	− 5.6
Total, 16 countries.	−1,643.8	− 19.8	+1,219.2	−262.8	−707.2

[a] Compiled from League of Nations, *Balances of Payments*, 1938, pp. 14-19, except as follows: Italy 1937, from unpublished memorandum by Al Costanzo; Germany 1937 and Austria 1929 and 1937, from unpublished memorandum by Werner Baer; the Netherlands, division between interest and dividends and other services 1929, based on unpublished memorandum by Erich Schiff; Yugoslavia 1936, from S. D. Obradovic, *La Politique Commerciale de la Yougoslavie* (Bergen Conference, 1939); Switzerland 1929, from Dorothy Grant Jacquelin, *Swiss-American Economic Relations* (1939), p. 196.

Note that in this table—and throughout the chapter—the plus and minus signs are used in the conventional balance of payments way. That is, the plus sign indicates transactions resulting in a net inflow of *foreign exchange* (or some equivalent), the minus sign a net outflow. Or, in bookkeeping terminology, the plus sign is used for "credit" transactions, and the minus sign for "debits."

As indicated above, figures given here for commodity trade have been corrected for wrong valuations and unrecorded trade, and therefore differ from the official trade data.

of the trade in commodities and services of all kinds. If the estimates were quite accurate—which undoubtedly they are not—this last column would also give a rough indication of the year's net change in the area's international debt and investment position. That is, it would indicate the net amount of new borrowing transactions (or net receipts from the sale of foreign assets) that had helped meet deficits in the trade and service accounts for some countries. Vice versa, it would indicate the net amount of new foreign investments (or repayments of existing obligations) that had been made possible as a result of the year's excess of receipts over payments in the trade and service accounts.[3]

Service transactions other than interest and dividends provided the principal means of payment for net imports of commodities. Shipping income was earned by most of the countries in the area,[4] and was particularly important in the case of Germany, France, Norway, the Netherlands, and Italy. The tourist trade was a source of income for many, and of notable proportions for France, Italy, and Switzerland. A few countries, however, usually found that their income from this trade was less than their own nationals spent on travel abroad. This group ordinarily included Denmark, Sweden, and Hungary, and also Germany in pre-depression days. Emigrant remittances were of outstanding importance in providing Italy with the foreign exchange

[3] The balance of payments statements for some of the countries also include estimates covering international borrowing and lending, or capital, transactions. But since such estimates are not available for all the countries in the area, it is impossible to include this item in the table. As indicated above, however, the balancing item in the trade and service accounts indicates the year's net change in the international debt and investment position of the area as a whole.

[4] The exceptions, as indicated by *Lloyd's Shipping Register*, were Bulgaria, Hungary, Albania, Austria, and Switzerland.

required for the purchase of imports, and were also relatively large in the case of Greece and Poland.

The payments that France and Germany, for example, usually made to migratory workers at harvest time, or during rush seasons in the coal industry, went principally to Poland and Italy, and therefore cancel out in the account for the area as a whole. About three-fourths of the reparation payments from Germany went to other countries within the area in 1929, and before 1937 such payments were discontinued. Earnings from the transit trade also were largely intra-area in character, while the net balance between receipts and payments for insurance and commissions was of small proportions.

In the aggregate, income from these several classes of service transactions (for 15 countries) amounted to 1.2 billion dollars in 1929, compared with net outgo of 1.5 billions on commodity trade account. In 1937 they provided 1.2 billions of net income, compared with a trade deficit of 1.3 billion dollars.

On balance the area imported gold in 1929, and exported a small amount in 1937. According to the table, net shipments and receipts of gold were relatively small in 1929, except in the case of France and Germany. France had stabilized her currency the year before. With a return of confidence in the domestic situation and a less optimistic outlook regarding conditions elsewhere, many of her people were bringing back some funds they had placed abroad a few years earlier. They were also making very few new investments in other countries. Germany was still making large reparation payments in 1929, borrowing funds wherever she could—principally on short term in the United States—but part of her trade and service payments were met by the shipment of gold.

By 1937 conditions in France had changed, and funds were again flowing out of the country for safekeeping. We cannot determine, from the balance of payments, whether this fugitive capital was transferred in gold or in the form of bills receivable on current trade and service account. But certainly, gold shipments which eventually reached the United States, via the Netherlands, played an important part in building up French balances in the United States.[5] The table does indicate, however, that not all the gold leaving France was available for investment. A considerable portion was required for meeting the deficit in the trade and service accounts. On the other hand, most of the gold shipped into the Netherlands played a part in the movement of capital from various European countries—temporarily placed in the Netherlands, on its way to the United States.

In the interest and dividend transactions of the area, a close balance has existed between payments and receipts. For the 15 countries for which we have data for both years, net *payments* amounted to 97 million dollars in 1929 compared with net *receipts* of 103 millions in 1937. Inclusion of the very considerable Swiss income from foreign investments reduces the net payments for 1929 to 20 million dollars, and probably would increase the net receipts for 1937 to something like 185 million dollars. As is well known, the area is made up of some creditor and some debtor countries, the one group holding a portion of the other's outstanding obligations. Also, the creditors have placed part of their foreign investments outside the area; and to a considerable extent the obligations of the debtors are held in outside countries.

United States securities and properties have long

[5] League of Nations, *Balances of Payments*, 1937, p. 29.

been a favored investment for some European countries, and during the 1920's Europe in turn received a large inflow of investment funds from the United States. This is common knowledge. What is not so generally known, however, is that in 1937 Nazi Europe, taken as a whole, was in a creditor position, vis-à-vis the United States. During the 1930's some countries of Europe had bought back their defaulted bonds at low prices, thereby reducing American claims against Europe; while others had invested heavily in American shares and bonds and industrial enterprises and built up short-term balances in American banks. In rough outline, the debt-investment situation in 1937 is shown by the accompanying table.

INVESTMENTS AND DEBTS OF NAZI EUROPE VS. THE UNITED STATES, 1937
(In millions of dollars)

Classes of Obligations	Nazi Europe's Investments in the United States[a]	American Investments in Nazi Europe[b]
Direct investments....................	503	876
Share holdings, common and preferred.....	1,551	811
Bonds...............................	377	
Miscellaneous........................	194	120
Total long term.....................	2,625	1,807
Short term[c].........................	756	242
Total..............................	3,381	2,049

[a] Paul D. Dickens (U. S. Dept. of Commerce), *Foreign Long-Term Investments in the United States*, 1937–39, p. 21.
[b] Long-term data are for 1938, and are based on U. S. Dept. of Commerce, *The Balance of International Payments of the United States*, 1938, p. 50; League of Nations, *Balances of Payments*, 1938, p. 146; Dickens, *American Direct Investments in Foreign Countries*, 1936, p. 9.
[c] Short-term data are from U. S. Treasury Dept., *Statistics of Capital Movements*, Report No. 6, p. 9.

Information concerning the area's debtor-creditor position elsewhere is quite incomplete. It has been estimated that British long-term investments on the

Continent amounted to about 1.4 billion dollars in 1937, but an offsetting estimate covering Nazi Europe's investment in Britain is not available.[6] German long-term investments inside the area amounted to not less than 650 million dollars in 1930, and the amount probably was larger than this in 1937.[7] The German long-term debt to foreigners amounted to about 5.3 billion dollars in 1935, of which 2.7 billions were intra-area debts, 2.1 billions were held in the United States and the United Kingdom (and are accounted for in the estimates given above for those countries), and a half billion was held elsewhere.[8] Dutch long-term investments abroad in 1937 amounted to 2.7 billion dollars, of which 600 millions were in other countries within the area.[9] Of Poland's foreign debts, about 450 million dollars were intra-area, 240 millions were held in the United States and the United Kingdom, and 190 millions held elsewhere.[10]

These various estimates covering long-term investments and debts may be summarized as follows for Nazi Europe:[11]

	Billion Dollars
Intra-area debts and investments.................	4.25
Investments in outside areas.....................	5.25
Liabilities to outside areas.......................	4.90

It will be seen, of course, that this summary state-

[6] Sir Robert Kindersley, *Economic Journal*, 1937, pp. 657–60. Of Kindersley's "unclassified" item, about 250 million dollars were probably in Europe. The same, 1933, pp. 199–202.

[7] *Wirtschaft und Statistik*, 1930, p. 893.

[8] League of Nations, *Balances of Payments*, 1937, p. 112.

[9] Erich Schiff, unpublished memorandum.

[10] Leopold Wellisz, *Foreign Capital in Poland* (1938), tables opposite p. 260.

[11] Figures for Norway show about 20 million dollars of investments inside the area, and small amounts of external debts. (League of Nations, *Balances of Payments*, 1937, pp. 162–63.) Figures for Estonia and Latvia show small amounts owed to German-area countries. (The same, pp. 95, 140.)

ment is quite incomplete. For example, it leaves out of account the French, Belgian, Swiss, and Swedish investments, and also the foreign indebtedness of Italy, the Balkans, etc.—except as they are covered by the various estimates given for other countries. With these items included, the totals for the three classes of debts and investments given here undoubtedly would be increased, but we have no basis for estimating the amounts involved.

On the whole, the trade and service accounts for 1937 show that there has been little slack between the foreign exchange receipts and payments of the area. This suggests that if there should be any future impairment of existing foreign-exchange resources, making the trade problem more difficult than it has been, or if the Hitler government should assume complete control over the area's economic life, it is quite likely that Nazi Europe would adopt the trading methods that Germany has followed in recent years. That is, an attempt probably would be made to bring commodity imports and exports into closer balance, by imposing and maintaining a wide range of controls over foreign trade and foreign exchange.

II. GERMAN METHODS OF BALANCING THE TRADE

During the depression, many countries adopted new methods of bringing their foreign exchange supply and demand into balance. Britain and the Netherlands both laid aside their traditional free-trade policies in favor of protective tariffs and, to get payment from their debtors, arranged clearing and payment agreements with them. Other countries raised their existing tariffs, or imposed quotas on various commodities, with a view to reducing imports. Throughout large areas, attempts were made at expanding domestic production—often at high costs—with a view to self-sufficiency in case of war, and to meet the unemployment, as well as the exchange, problem. Export promotion plans were put into effect. But in no other country was foreign trade subject to such varied and far-reaching controls as those employed in Germany.

With the cessation of foreign lending early in 1931, the problem of financing imports assumed a major role in German trade policy. For a few years the measures taken brought a decrease in imports.[12] Soon after the Hitler government came into power, in 1933, it adopted a policy of increasing employment within Germany, and of building up the war machine. Thereafter, the promotion of exports became one of several means employed in making possible the required increase in raw material imports.

Under the "New Plan," introduced in the fall of 1934, no imports are permitted without a license, which may be issued—or refused—by one of the many supervisory offices to which this authority has been delegated.[13] As the plan worked before the war, these offices, in arriving at decisions, kept in mind the general economic policy of the government—which gave preference to imports of raw materials for rearmament or re-export purposes, as compared with goods intended for civilian consumption. What materials were taken into the country for

[12] In 1932–34, the government rationed foreign exchange on a percentage basis; and when the "New Plan" was introduced, the rationing quota had declined to 5 per cent. Howard S. Ellis, *Exchange Control in Central Europe* (1941), p. 204. On the crisis of 1931 and the policies adopted by the government see also C. R. S. Harris, *Germany's Foreign Indebtedness* (1935), particularly Chaps. II, IV, V.

[13] Before the outbreak of the present war, there were 27 such offices, each in charge of a group of commodities.

rearmament purposes is not shown by the trade figures, as it has been the policy of the government to omit from the published reports all information concerning the volume and value of "hidden imports of war stocks."[14] Omission of these imports leads to an overstatement of Germany's net receipts and receivables on trade and service account—for example, in the table on page 133— and therefore tends to exaggerate the success that actually was achieved in balancing the accounts under the New Plan.

From 1934 forward, Germany followed a policy of stimulating exports for the purpose of increasing imports. To this end, many new measures were invented and put in practice. Rather than lower prices in the domestic market, Hitler decided upon subsidies as a method of export promotion. Cash subsidies were given to some exporters who were facing strong competition in foreign markets. Other exporters were subsidized through the permission given them to buy abroad (and resell in Germany, at a big profit) outstanding dollar bonds representing earlier American loans to Germany. Through bilateral trade agreements, countries from which Germany bought its food and raw materials were forced to buy German goods in return. A complicated system of exchange controls was gradually developed, under which there was a variety of rates, each applying to special "kinds" of reichsmarks, or mark balances—used in meeting special kinds of foreign obligations. A very small proportion of the trade was handled through direct barter.

Fashioned to meet all kinds of contingencies, these

---

[14] *Annual Economic Review*, Germany, 1938, p. 10. This means that the published data understate the volume and value of imports, and show an export balance larger than was actually realized in the commodity trade.

controls were varied in character and intricate in detail. To operate them, as they developed, hundreds of boards were created, thousands of officials employed. The brief consideration given these measures here can do little more than suggest the maze of helps and hindrances and bewildering red tape in which German business was operating during the late 1930's.

In general, under the cash subsidy plan, grants were made to individual exporters to enable them to underbid foreigners competing against them on particular contracts. Here, as in other sections of the export-promotion plan, the amount of aid given was determined by the differences between the German cost price (plus a "fair profit") and the foreign price asked from a potential purchaser. Funds for the purpose were provided from a turnover tax which the government collected from industry.

The dollar-bond plan provided subsidies for German exporters at the expense of foreign holders. These German bonds—on which interest continued to be paid in Germany, though not transferable outside the country—were selling at or near par in Germany before the outbreak of the present war, but at very low prices elsewhere. By receiving permission to take these bonds in part payment for his goods, therefore, the German exporter was enabled to make a profit on the bond transaction to offset a loss in connection with the sale of his goods.

The several types of bilateral trade agreements negotiated by Germany included clearing agreements, payment agreements, compensation agreements, and agreements transacted by means of the "aski" mark. Moreover, in Germany's trade, service, and financial transactions with other countries, she made use of many combinations and variations of these principal types. The characteristic common to most of them was this: the credits accruing to one of the signatory countries for commodities exported, or services rendered to the other country, could be used in no way except as payment for imports of goods and services from that country.

Under the clearing agreements, the two countries concerned handled their trade on a bookkeeping basis, without any actual transfer of funds from one agreement country to the other. In the payment agreements, on the other hand, all payments were made currently in *devisen*[15]—the agreement specifying that payment should pass through a special agency in each country, to ensure compliance with all terms of the agreement. In compensation transactions, as in clearing, there was no transfer of *devisen*, but instead of the periodic balancing of all items in the accounts provided for under clearing agreements, each lot of exports was immediately offset by an import of equal value, practically reducing trade to direct barter.[16] Under the aski-mark plan, the German importer paid for his purchases in marks—but the foreign exporter taking such aski marks could not use them in trade with any outside country except Germany, and in Germany could use them only in ways specified by the German government. Moreover, the value of these mark payments was determined, in large part, by actions which the German government took in connection with the authorization of imports and exports under this scheme, rather than by the interplay of forces in a free foreign-exchange market.[17]

[15] Foreign currency and foreign exchange, free of any controls regarding its use.

[16] Ellis, *Exchange Control in Central Europe*, pp. 13–15. Ellis classifies the aski-mark transactions as a subclass of compensation transactions.

[17] The controls exercised over prices in the German market provided the

In addition to the aski marks, there were various other types of "blocked marks"—marks belonging to the foreign creditors of Germany, but not transferable to them. In the hands of German consumers all marks were of equal value. Outside Germany, however, blocked currency sold at only a fraction of the rate quoted for the government-supported "free exchange marks." These blocked marks, like the depreciated dollar bonds, were sometimes brought into the government's plan for subsidizing exports, and added their bit to the confusing picture of German trade.

Finally, the "free mark," which was not permitted to depreciate, was the mark in which Germany calculated her outstanding indebtedness to her foreign creditors, and the mark in which her commodity trade was calculated and recorded.[18] With quotations for this unit kept at par, the government was able to maintain the illusion that there had been no depreciation in the German currency. This was an important point in the program followed during the thirties, for the German people still remembered the postwar period of inflation.

Since the outbreak of hostilities, considerable attention has been given to the problem of maintaining the value of the German currency. A policy has been followed of limiting its use to the old Reich and the provinces recently incorporated in it. Even the "occupation marks," used to provide means of payment for German troops during the invasion of neighboring countries, are

government with one means of manipulating the aski-mark rate. Hans J. Dernburg, "The Principles of the German Foreign Trade System," *Denison Economic Review*, April 1940, p. 13. The value of other types of "blocked marks" also depended primarily on government controls and policies.

[18] By the fact that the free mark was kept at par, a smaller number of marks was required to meet payments into blocked accounts on dollar, sterling, and other foreign obligations.

being gradually withdrawn from circulation. In most cases, the troops are now being paid in the local currency of the countries where they are stationed. More direct means of maintaining the value of the mark have also been adopted. By recent agreements with the governments of a number of countries in the German-controlled area, the exchange value of the mark has been arbitrarily increased in terms of the currencies of those countries. And by a decree of November 22, 1940, the Reichsmark was proclaimed equal to the "gold-mark"—although the reserves of the Reichsbank provide only a 0.55 per cent gold cover for it. Meantime, the German government continues to exercise strict control over trade with other countries in the area and over the greatly reduced volume of external trade.

Without considering the German trade plan in detail, or attempting any evaluation of it, one may readily say that under it trade with foreign countries has become a cumbersome process. Certainly it would have to be altered in many ways before it could be applied to the larger area of Nazi Europe. For example, various adjustments would be required if the component states of the area are to retain their present, or other separate, currency systems. However, consideration of the many questions that would be involved in shaping the German plan to fit the larger area are outside the scope of this study.

CHAPTER VI

NAZI EUROPE'S PLACE IN WORLD TRADE

Preceding chapters have indicated the volume of Nazi Europe's requirements for the more important foodstuffs and raw materials. In that connection they have also given fragmentary pictures of the German area's place in world trade. The present chapter will consider the aggregate trade of the area, showing how it has been distributed among various sources and markets, and the importance of this commerce to the nations concerned. Throughout the chapter comparisons are in value terms, in contrast with the tonnage data given in Chapters II–IV. Figures reported in the many currencies of the world have been converted to United States dollars at current rates of exchange, thus reducing them all to comparable terms.

I. WHERE EUROPE TRADED

It goes without saying that the trade of Nazi Europe involves transactions with all parts of the world. Also, of course, a considerable fraction of the trade is intra-area in character. In fact, both in 1937 and 1929, half of the total reported was trade between the several countries of the area; half was with outside sources and markets.

In the aggregate, the area's trade with the British Isles has been larger than with any other single country or continent. This is shown for 1929 and 1937 by the table and map on pages 147–48. Britain also enjoyed the distinction in 1937 of being the only large trade region that bought more in Nazi Europe than it sold. In 1929,

Africa too was a net importer from the Continent, but by 1937 this had changed and Africa, like most of the other large world areas, was a net exporter in its trade with Nazi Europe. Almost 31 per cent of the area's exports to outside markets were to the British Isles in 1929, and 30 per cent in 1937.

NAZI EUROPE'S TRADE WITH LARGE WORLD AREAS, 1937, 1929[a]

(Commodity trade, in millions of dollars)[b]

Source of Imports Destination of Exports	1937			1929		
	Imports	Exports	Net	Imports	Exports	Net
British Isles...........	873	1,225	−352	1,205	1,826	−621
Russian area..........	377	322	+ 55	505	489	+ 16
Africa................	813	685	+128	693	733	− 40
Asia.................	955	642	+313	1,058	812	+246
Oceania..............	189	68	+121	263	111	+152
United States.........	768	574	+194	1,581	956	+625
Other Western Hemisphere..............	1,117	605	+512	1,419	879	+540
All outside areas.......	5,092	4,121	+971	6,724	5,806	+918
Intra-area trade.......	4,516	4,516	—	6,266	6,266	—
Total trade...........	9,608	8,637	+971	12,990	12,072	+918

[a] Throughout this chapter, both the import and export figures are based on the official *import* data of the importing countries. In this way the total for world exports is made exactly equal to that for world imports. This would not be the case if our export figures were compiled from *reported exports*. Further discussion of this point will be found in App. A, p. 187. Figures for 1937 were compiled from U. S. Dept. of Commerce, *Foreign Commerce Yearbook*, 1938 and for 1929 from *Commerce Yearbook*, Vol. II, 1930, 1931, supplemented by the official trade reports of all political subdivisions of the world.

[b] In a very few cases, shipments of bullion and specie could not be segregated from the commodity trade.

Trade with the United States was second in importance in 1929, but ranked considerably lower in 1937. That is, during the 1930's Nazi Europe's trade with the United States declined in relation to the total trade of the area—and also in aggregate amount. The

WHERE NAZI EUROPE BOUGHT AND SOLD GOODS IN 1937
(Figures are in millions of dollars)

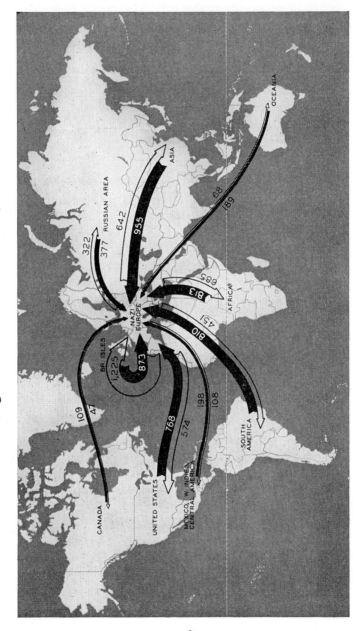

greatest decline was shown for imports from the United States. In 1929 these amounted to 1,581 million dollars, or 24 per cent of all German-area imports from outside sources, and in 1937 to only 768 millions, or 15 per cent of the total. This compares with a shrinkage in the area's total imports from outside sources, from 6,724 million dollars in 1929 to 5,092 millions in 1937.[1]

The trade of the several countries of Nazi Europe varies widely as regards source and destination. The tables on pages 150–53 give the geographic distribution of trade for each of the countries in the area.

Germany's aggregate trade—the largest for any of the 20 countries—shifted toward intra-area countries during the thirties. By 1937 it was divided almost equally between intra-area and external trade. In both years Germany was a net exporter to countries inside the area, and a net importer from outside countries. In 1929 her trade with the United States was of outstanding importance, being almost as large as that with all other Western Hemisphere countries combined, and almost as large as that with all countries of the Far East. By 1937, however, her trade with the United States was smaller than with any other region given in the table. In the area's trade with the British Isles, Germany stood first in 1929, and in 1937 was second only to Denmark.

For France, the commercial nation of second importance on the Continent, transactions with Africa were larger than with any other outside country or continent. In the main, of course, this trade was with her nearby

[1] Reference to the figures given in earlier chapters indicate that in part this represented an actual shrinkage in the volume of world trade, in part merely the general fall in world prices. The effect of the price change, however, is partially offset by the fact that the American dollar, the currency in which the trade is expressed, had depreciated in value between 1929 and 1937.

NAZI EUROPE'S FOREIGN TRADE IN 1937[a]
(In millions of dollars)

I. DESTINATION OF EXPORTS

Countries (By groups)	British Isles	Russian Area	Africa	Asia and Oceania	United States	Other Western Hemisphere	Total External	Intra-Area	Total
I. Bulgaria	5.0	2.1	1.2	.4	1.9	—	10.6	49.0	59.6
Rumania	21.9	2.2	14.7	12.7	5.0	.1	56.6	219.0	275.6
Yugoslavia	12.2	1.6	4.8	.8	6.2	2.1	27.7	139.5	167.2
Total	39.1	5.9	20.7	13.9	13.1	2.2	94.9	407.5	502.4
II. Denmark	182.2	12.1	2.7	2.8	6.8	6.8	213.4	126.4	339.8
Hungary	11.8	3.0	4.9	2.6	5.5	1.8	29.6	135.6	165.2
Netherlands	152.5	36.6	22.7	79.3	53.3	42.5	386.9	317.8	704.7
Half of Poland[b]	27.1	3.6	2.1	3.4	9.8	4.3	50.3	80.0	130.3
Portugal	21.1	1.9	11.6	2.1	8.8	6.7	52.2	37.5	89.7
Spain	49.5	5.4	6.4	3.1	13.8	8.9	87.1	82.7	169.8
Total	444.2	62.6	50.4	93.3	98.0	71.0	819.5	780.0	1,599.5
III. Albania	—	—	—	—	.1	—	.1	3.8	3.9
Greece	10.6	3.0	2.5	1.3	17.2	.9	35.5	58.0	93.5
Norway	54.9	7.3	7.6	15.1	26.0	8.3	119.2	113.2	232.4
Sweden	131.3	33.3	13.5	37.6	58.7	25.3	299.7	256.0	555.7
Total	196.8	43.6	23.6	54.0	102.0	34.5	454.5	431.0	885.5
IV. Germany	179.6	118.5	83.3	302.0	92.5	266.8	1,042.7	1,257.7	2,300.4
Austria	12.9	8.9	4.2	12.6	5.8	4.9	49.3	182.8	232.1
Belgium-Luxemburg	121.0	37.6	63.1	74.1	75.1	78.3	449.2	426.7	875.9
Czechoslovakia	36.1	14.1	18.0	24.2	37.2	17.4	147.0	241.7	388.7
France	122.5	17.5	249.0	77.0	75.6	66.5	608.1	394.7	1,002.8
Italy	37.4	6.8	166.2	34.4	48.2	45.8	338.8	232.2	571.0
Switzerland	34.8	6.8	6.5	24.4	26.9	17.8	117.2	161.8	279.0
Total	544.3	210.2	590.3	548.7	361.3	497.5	2,752.3	2,897.6	5,649.9
Total Nazi Europe	1,224.4	322.3	685.0	709.9	574.4	605.2	4,121.2	4,516.1	8,637.3

II. SOURCE OF IMPORTS (1937)

I. Bulgaria...................	3.0	1.7	.5	1.2	1.3	.1	7.8	55.4	63.2
Rumania...................	13.9	1.7	6.3	1.9	5.8	.1	29.7	118.3	148.0
Yugoslavia................	9.4	.7	2.0	4.7	7.2	4.4	28.4	91.7	120.1
Total................	26.3	4.1	8.8	7.8	14.3	4.6	65.9	265.4	331.3
II. Denmark................	140.7	10.9	3.0	5.6	19.2	17.2	196.6	170.0	366.6
Hungary.................	7.4	1.3	3.5	3.4	6.3	2.5	24.4	115.4	139.8
Netherlands..............	71.4	43.1	28.8	119.4	75.0	107.5	445.2	403.4	848.6
Half of Poland[b].........	14.2	2.0	6.8	13.1	14.1	8.9	59.1	58.6	117.7
Portugal.................	19.3	.6	11.7	5.6	10.9	4.2	52.3	45.0	97.3
Spain....................	14.0	19.5	.9	.4	6.0	4.1	44.9	76.2	121.1
Total................	267.0	77.4	54.7	147.5	131.5	144.4	822.5	868.6	1,691.1
III. Albania................	.3	—	.1	.5	.3	.1	1.3	4.6	5.9
Greece...................	15.1	3.8	3.3	6.3	5.9	14.8	49.2	88.3	137.5
Norway..................	58.8	12.9	4.9	20.9	27.4	31.3	156.2	161.3	317.5
Sweden..................	72.2	23.8	6.4	38.7	75.0	58.4	274.5	259.8	534.3
Total................	146.4	40.5	14.7	66.4	108.6	104.6	481.2	514.0	995.2
IV. Germany...............	127.9	105.4	160.7	335.2	113.5	393.6	1,236.3	945.4	2,181.7
Austria..................	12.3	7.6	7.0	21.2	16.4	12.3	76.8	195.5	272.3
Belgium-Luxemburg.......	78.5	45.7	93.4	100.8	80.5	121.1	520.0	397.7	917.7
Czechoslovakia..........	24.7	11.4	19.0	45.7	33.6	24.8	159.2	223.3	382.5
France..................	136.0	59.8	376.2	303.1	160.7	177.8	1,213.6	483.9	1,697.5
Italy....................	28.6	17.2	65.6	92.0	79.5	96.4	379.3	346.6	725.9
Switzerland.............	25.7	8.2	12.4	24.2	28.9	37.5	136.9	275.7	412.6
Total................	433.7	255.3	734.3	922.2	513.1	863.5	3,722.1	2,868.1	6,590.2..
Total Nazi Europe........	873.4	377.3	812.5	1,143.9	767.5	1,117.1	5,091.7	4,516.1	9,607.8

[a] Sources of the data, and questions of method and definition, are considered in footnotes to the table on p. 147 and in App. A.
[b] Half of the trade of Poland (and Danzig) is included with Nazi Europe, half with the Russian area.

NAZI EUROPE'S FOREIGN TRADE IN 1929[a]
(In millions of dollars)

I. DESTINATION OF EXPORTS

Countries (By groups)	British Isles	Russian Area	Africa	Asia and Oceania	United States	Other Western Hemisphere	Total External	Intra-Area	Total
I. Bulgaria	.4	.8	.8	1.1	.9	.6	4.0	31.8	35.8
Rumania	13.9	1.6	12.5	6.9	.6	—	36.1	154.8	190.9
Yugoslavia	2.9	.5	4.1	.6	2.3	3.5	13.9	111.9	125.8
Total	17.2	2.9	17.4	8.6	3.8	4.1	54.0	298.5	352.5
Denmark	271.2	15.8	.9	6.6	4.6	5.9	305.0	168.1	473.1
Hungary	3.3	2.0	1.4	5.2	1.8	.2	13.9	141.6	155.0
Netherlands	204.2	18.8	27.2	126.9	83.9	63.0	524.0	471.0	995.5
Half of Poland[b]	16.6	12.6	2.1	2.1	2.4	.8	35.4	128.5	163.9
Portugal	20.2	.5	11.2	.8	7.3	8.9	48.9	35.8	84.7
Spain	103.0	4.8	10.5	3.8	36.1	50.8	209.0	175.0	384.0
Total	618.5	54.5	52.1	145.4	136.1	129.6	1,136.2	1,120.0	2,256.2
III. Albania	—	—	—	.1	—	—	.1	2.9	3.0
Greece	12.9	.4	4.8	1.2	17.8	.8	37.9	60.7	98.6
Norway	66.7	7.9	3.3	14.1	21.2	12.4	125.6	106.6	232.2
Sweden	125.8	29.9	13.7	29.6	53.0	21.3	273.3	247.8	521.1
Total	205.4	38.2	21.8	45.0	92.0	34.5	436.9	418.0	854.9
IV. Germany	329.4	269.2	89.4	311.6	254.7	287.5	1,541.8	1,872.5	3,414.3
Austria	12.5	22.9	4.8	12.5	12.2	3.6	68.5	235.0	303.5
Belgium-Luxemburg	215.4	13.9	67.6	88.2	74.0	108.9	568.0	509.7	1,077.7
Czechoslovakia	30.9	29.6	12.3	22.9	46.1	8.9	150.7	381.7	532.4
France	258.6	36.3	393.9	157.0	171.5	160.5	1,177.8	843.1	2,020.9
Italy	76.9	11.0	64.4	91.0	117.1	118.6	479.0	343.8	822.8
Switzerland	61.5	10.4	9.7	40.7	48.4	22.8	193.5	243.7	437.2
Total	985.2	393.3	642.1	723.9	724.0	710.8	4,179.3	4,429.5	8,608.8
Total Nazi Europe	1,826.3	488.9	733.4	922.9	955.9	879.0	5,806.4	6,266.0	12,072.4

II. SOURCE OF IMPORTS (1929)

							Total Nazi Europe		Total
I. Bulgaria	5.3	.4	.5	1.9	2.0	—	10.1	49.8	59.9
Rumania	12.9	4.8	2.9	1.8	10.7	—	33.1	141.3	174.4
Yugoslavia	7.5	1.7	.3	4.6	6.3	5.2	25.6	108.0	133.6
Total	25.7	6.9	3.7	8.3	19.0	5.2	68.8	299.1	367.9
II. Denmark	70.6	20.6	2.6	25.3	64.1	19.3	202.5	274.3	476.8
Hungary	5.2	4.8	1.4	4.0	8.6	.3	24.3	161.5	185.8
Netherlands	104.1	39.6	25.9	103.1	109.4	133.4	515.5	584.1	1,099.6
Half of Poland[b]	14.9	3.3	2.1	8.7	21.5	6.8	57.3	116.3	173.6
Portugal	30.3	—	8.2	.1	15.2	4.9	58.7	52.9	111.6
Spain	68.9	18.1	20.7	38.9	84.1	69.1	299.8	208.3	508.1
Total	294.0	86.4	60.9	180.1	302.9	233.8	1,158.1	1,397.4	2,555.5
III. Albania	.5	—			.7	—	1.6	5.8	7.4
Greece	21.5	3.8	4.4	11.1	27.0	14.6	82.4	88.1	170.5
Norway	62.6	5.8	.8	6.8	30.1	18.7	124.8	160.6	285.4
Sweden	82.8	11.8	1.1	6.2	70.1	32.1	204.1	272.0	476.1
Total	167.4	21.4	6.7	24.1	127.9	65.4	412.9	526.5	939.4
IV. Germany	206.6	214.6	162.4	465.6	426.5	457.9	1,933.6	1,261.9	3,195.5
Austria	13.1	24.4	4.2	18.5	27.9	14.1	102.2	354.2	456.4
Belgium-Luxemburg	109.9	37.2	63.3	55.8	93.8	109.2	469.2	519.2	988.4
Czechoslovakia	27.2	30.3	16.0	49.5	68.6	40.0	231.6	355.8	587.4
France	229.7	55.3	313.6	362.3	280.7	292.5	1,534.1	739.8	2,273.9
Italy	106.8	22.6	47.5	131.8	187.3	156.2	652.6	458.2	1,110.8
Switzerland	24.7	6.1	14.5	24.6	46.2	44.7	160.8	353.9	514.7
Total	718.0	390.5	621.5	1,108.1	1,131.0	1,115.0	5,084.1	4,043.0	9,127.1
Total Nazi Europe	1,205.1	505.2	692.8	1,320.6	1,580.8	1,419.4	6,723.9	6,266.0	12,989.9

a Sources of the data, and questions of method and definition, are considered in footnotes to the table on p. 147 and in App. A.
b Half of the trade of Poland (and Danzig) is included with Nazi Europe, half with the Russian area.

colony, Algeria, which from many points of view is part of metropolitan France. Her trade with the United States in both years almost equalled that with all other Western Hemisphere countries combined.

The Balkan countries, without exception, traded more largely within the area than with outside countries. In the Baltic group, the dairying countries had their principal trade with the British Isles. Norway and Sweden both divided their trade about evenly between the intra-area and outside countries—about half of their external trade being with the British Isles. All of the food-exporting countries (Groups I and II in the table) sold much more to Britain than they bought from those islands.

Italy's principal external trade in 1929 was with the United States. In 1937, however, her trade with the United States declined more than 50 per cent, while trade with Africa more than doubled, putting the latter in first place.

II. NAZI EUROPE'S PLACE IN WESTERN HEMISPHERE TRADE

In Western Hemisphere countries, as in the rest of the world, trade with continental Europe has long been accepted as a traditional and necessary economic activity. At the present time, however, this trade is badly disrupted and uncertainty clouds the future. At the best, impoverished Europe is likely to find her capacity to buy abroad considerably reduced. At the worst, there is the threat that Western Hemisphere countries may face sharp bargaining in a world where the trade of all German-controlled countries is vested in a single agency. However, it is not our purpose to explore this question here. What we shall consider is the relative importance of the German area in Western Hemisphere trade in 1929 and 1937.

Nazi Europe has been the largest consumer of Western Hemisphere goods. That is to say, the countries of German-controlled Europe buy a larger proportion of Western Hemisphere exports than any other country or continent. In the import trade of the New World, however, the case has sometimes been different. In 1929, the United States was the principal source of imports, slightly exceeding Nazi Europe in its exports to the other Americas. This is shown by the table below.

WESTERN HEMISPHERE TRADE WITH LARGE WORLD AREAS, 1937, 1929[a]
(In millions of dollars)

Destination of Exports Source of Imports	1937			1929		
	Exports	Imports	Net[b]	Exports	Imports	Net[b]
Nazi Europe....	1,884.6	1,179.6	− 705.0	3,000.2	1,834.9	−1,165.3
British Isles.....	1,616.8	608.9	−1,007.9	1,825.5	935.5	− 890.0
Russian area....	134.1	74.0	− 60.1	176.0	49.2	− 126.8
Africa..........	210.0	110.6	− 99.4	199.3	112.5	− 86.8
Asia............	747.1	1,123.7	+ 376.6	828.6	1,397.6	+ 569.0
Oceania........	163.2	93.8	− 69.4	272.7	81.6	− 191.1
All outside areas.	4,755.8	3,190.6	−1,565.2	6,302.3	4,411.3	−1,891.0
United States...	1,111.6	1,104.3	− 7.3	1,620.6	1,891.1	+ 270.5
South America..	504.1	725.7	+ 221.6	816.9	979.7	+ 162.8
Other American countries[c].....	1,013.1	798.8	− 214.3	1,534.3	1,101.0	− 433.3
All inter-American trade...	2,628.8	2,628.8	0.0	3,971.8	3,971.8	0.0
Total.........	7,384.6	5,819.4	−1,565.2	10,274.1	8,383.1	−1,891.0

[a] Sources of the data, and questions of method and definition, are considered in footnotes to the table on p. 147 and in App. A.
[b] Net imports (+), net exports (−).
[c] Other North America, Central America, and the West Indies.

Among the large trade areas outside the New World, the British Isles ranked second as a market for Western Hemisphere exports. Asia stood second as a source of imports. Trade with other large world areas—the Russian group, Africa, and Oceania—was very small.

WESTERN HEMISPHERE TRADE WITH

(Dollar figures

I. IN 1937

Western Hemi-sphere Countries	Western Hemi-sphere Exports		Western Hemi-sphere Imports		Trade with Europe as Percentage of Total	
	To Europe	Total	From Europe	Total	Ex-ports	Im-ports
United States.....	$ 767.5	$ 3,408.3	$ 574.4	$3,081.0	22.5	18.6
Canada and New-foundland.......	108.9	1,145.8	46.7	832.3	9.5	5.6
Total..........	$ 876.4	$ 4,554.1	$ 621.1	$3,913.3	19.2	15.9
Mexico...........	$ 52.3	$ 144.6	$ 46.2	$ 173.6	36.2	26.6
British West Indies and British Hon-durasᵇ..........	7.2ᶜ	85.9	4.1	92.6	8.4	4.4
Other Central America........	28.7	70.4	19.1	72.2	40.8	26.5
Cuba.............	11.6	186.9	17.0	129.3	6.2	13.1
Other West Indies.	98.2	260.2	21.2	197.9	37.7	10.7
Total..........	$ 198.0	$ 748.0	$ 107.6	$ 665.6	26.5	16.2
Ecuador..........	9.6	18.9	4.1	11.0	50.8	37.3
Colombia........	31.7	98.3	25.9	95.6	32.2	27.1
Venezuela.........	27.2	192.2	27.0	85.5	14.2	31.6
British Guiana....	2.9ᶜ	15.2	0.3	9.9	19.1	3.0
Dutch and French Guiana..	2.6	6.4	3.6	4.6	40.6	78.3
Argentina.........	418.1	955.3	185.8	482.2	43.8	38.5
Bolivia...........	12.7	33.7	5.2	21.4	37.7	24.3
Brazil............	161.1	383.6	133.0	330.1	42.0	40.3
Chile.............	80.3	187.9	31.4	88.3	42.7	35.6
Paraguay.........	4.2	7.8	1.7	8.0	53.8	21.3
Peru.............	35.4	111.7	19.5	59.4	31.7	32.8
Uruguay..........	24.4	71.5	13.4	44.5	34.1	30.1
Total..........	$ 810.2	$ 2,082.5	$ 450.9	$1,240.5	38.9	36.3
Total Western Hemisphere.....	$1,884.6	$ 7,384.6	$1,179.6	$5,819.4	25.5	20.3

ᵃ Sources of the data, and questions of method and definition, are considered in footnotes to the table on p. 147 and in App. A.

ᵇ Bermuda is included with the British West Indies, and the inter-island trade of the group is treated as "domestic" trade.

NAZI EUROPE, AND THE WORLD, 1937, 1929[a]
are in millions)

II. IN 1929

Western Hemisphere Countries	Western Hemisphere Exports		Western Hemisphere Imports		Trade with Europe as Percentage of Total	
	To Europe	Total	From Europe	Total	Exports	Imports
United States.....	$1,580.8	$ 5,654.4	$ 955.9	$4,395.6	28.0	21.7
Canada and New-foundland.......	229.5	1,164.4	94.9	1,329.8	19.7	7.1
Total..........	$1,810.3	$ 6,818.8	$1,050.8	$5,725.4	26.5	18.4
Mexico..........	$ 46.0	$ 195.5	$ 38.0	$ 184.5	23.5	20.6
British West Indies and British Honduras[b]......	28.7	93.9	5.0	90.4	30.6	5.5
Other Central America........	56.4	116.4	21.8	105.8	48.5	20.6
Cuba............	22.5	281.7	39.0	215.3	8.0	18.1
Other West Indies.	48.2	162.3	23.0	191.6	29.7	12.0
Total..........	$ 201.8	$ 849.8	$ 126.8	$ 787.6	23.7	16.1
Ecuador..........	5.2	15.5	5.9	16.8	33.5	35.1
Colombia........	14.6	138.4	40.8	121.2	10.5	33.7
Venezuela.........	38.0	217.8	26.5	87.2	17.4	30.4
British Guiana....	1.4	10.1	0.6	10.6	13.9	5.7
Dutch and French Guiana ..	0.8	2.3	3.4	4.6	34.8	73.9
Argentina.........	586.4	1,214.2	317.0	815.5	48.3	38.9
Bolivia...........	3.2	32.9	6.4	24.9	9.7	25.7
Brazil............	180.5	480.6	138.0	413.5	37.6	33.4
Chile............	118.7	289.9	64.0	194.7	40.9	32.9
Paraguay.........	1.2	8.8	3.5	12.7	13.6	27.6
Peru.............	7.0	106.2	21.4	75.6	6.6	28.3
Uruguay..........	31.1	88.8	29.8	92.8	35.0	32.1
Total..........	$ 988.1	$ 2,605.5	$ 657.3	$1,870.1	37.9	35.1
Total Western Hemisphere.....	$3,000.2	$10,274.1	$1,834.9	$8,383.1	29.2	21.9

[c] Imports from British Guiana into Germany are included in the total for British West Indies and British Honduras.

The individual countries of the Western Hemisphere vary widely as regards their trade relations with Europe. This statement applies both to the value of this trade and to its relative importance. For example, Paraguay's exports to Europe in 1937 amounted to 4.2 million dollars and imports to 1.7 millions, while for the United States the corresponding exports were 768 million dollars and imports 574 millions. Also, in 1937 Cuba sent Europe only 6 per cent of her total exports; Paraguay sent 54 per cent. These and other comparisons of this sort may be read from the table on pages 156–57.

As the table shows, five of the ten South American republics sent as much as 40 per cent of their exports to Europe in 1937, though only two were in this group in 1929. This trade included a large proportion of the coffee, cotton, and rubber exported from Brazil; grain, wool, linseed, and meat from Argentina; coffee and oil from Colombia; copper from Chile and Peru; oil from Venezuela (via Aruba and Curacao in the Dutch West Indies); and of various other products of smaller aggregate value. Here the present wartime interruption of the flow of trade disturbs the whole economy of the countries concerned. The prospect of any enforced shifts to other markets—or other products—raises questions of grave concern.

The problem of the import trade is one of minor importance as compared with the problem of markets. It is true that seven South American republics bought as much as 30 per cent of their imports in Europe in 1937—and seven in 1929—but this trade could readily be shifted to other sources of supply. The difficulty is to find new markets for exports, particularly for such abundant commodities as coffee and grain, and thereby to acquire the funds needed for the import trade.

Trade with the German area is not so important for the United States as it is for many South American countries. Some 23 per cent of our exports went to Nazi Europe in 1937, and 19 per cent of our imports came from there. This means that all other trade areas, in the aggregate, accounted for 77 per cent of our exports and for 81 per cent of our imports. A comparison of the import and export trade of the United States with Europe and with other large areas is given in the accompanying table.

TRADE OF THE UNITED STATES WITH LARGE WORLD AREAS, 1937, 1929[a]
(In millions of dollars)

Destination of Exports, Source of Imports	1937			1929		
	Exports	Imports	Net[b]	Exports	Imports	Net[b]
Nazi Europe...	767.5	574.4	−193.1	1,580.8	955.9	− 624.9
British Isles....	539.5	204.6	−334.9	916.8	334.1	− 582.7
Russian area...	88.6	61.1	− 27.5	144.7	41.6	− 103.1
Africa.........	160.7	92.0	− 68.7	155.6	108.0	− 47.6
Asia..........	642.2	968.9	+326.7	744.7	1,278.9	+ 534.2
Oceania.......	105.5	68.4	− 37.1	220.7	56.5	− 164.2
South America.	311.7	421.9	+110.2	590.3	639.7	+ 49.4
Other American countries[c]..	792.6	689.7	−102.9	1,300.8	980.9	− 319.9
Total........	3,408.3	3,081.0	−327.3	5,654.4	4,395.6	−1,258.8

[a] Sources of the data, and questions of method and definition, are considered in footnotes to the table on p. 147 and in App. A.
[b] Net imports (+), net exports (−).
[c] Other North America, Central America, and the West Indies.

While in 1929 Nazi Europe was the principal market for our exports, in 1937 it ranked second to the group of countries shown in the table under the caption of "Other American countries." In the import trade of the United States, it was the area of third importance— Asia being the most important source of supply, and "Other American countries" second. Imports from South America exceeded those from Britain, while exports to Britain were larger than those to South America.

III. NAZI EUROPE'S PLACE IN EASTERN HEMISPHERE TRADE

If by some magic the countries of Nazi Europe were all wiped off the map and their trade obliterated, the shock would scarcely register on the economic seismographs of a few countries. In others it would be followed by terrific dislocations of both trade and industry —as now actually threatens in some areas, as a result of the British blockade. In short, the countries of the world vary widely in the extent to which their trade is integrated with that of Europe. This has already been indicated for the countries of the Western Hemisphere, and it applies with even greater force to those in the other half of the world.

In the trade of the British Isles, Nazi Europe has normally ranked above all other countries and continents. In 1937, for example, it provided a market for more British goods than any other two continents combined, and for four times the amount taken by the United States. Also, it supplied Britain with imports valued at more than twice those shipped from the United States, and 14 per cent greater than the total from all Western Hemisphere countries except the United States. This may be seen from the accompanying table, page 161.

The lower section of the table shows the trade of the British Isles with all Empire countries, with Nazi Europe, and with all other foreign countries. Grouped in this way, the figures indicate that Nazi Europe had been losing ground to Empire countries in the import trade of the British Isles. In 1929, Nazi Europe supplied 32 per cent of Britain's imports; all Empire countries together, only 29 per cent. By 1937, the area's share had fallen to 25 per cent, compared with 39 per cent for Empire sources.

TRADE OF THE UNITED KINGDOM AND EIRE, 1937, 1929[a]
(In millions of dollars)

I. WITH LARGE WORLD AREAS

Destination of Exports Source of Imports	1937			1929		
	Exports	Imports	Net[b]	Exports	Imports	Net[b]
Nazi Europe......	873.4	1,224.4	+ 351.0	1,205.1	1,826.3	+ 621.2
Russian area......	115.6	320.4	+ 204.8	77.9	241.7	+ 163.8
Africa............	410.0	327.0	− 83.0	424.0	334.6	− 89.4
Asia.............	452.3	622.4	+ 170.1	808.9	567.2	− 241.7
Oceania..........	325.0	550.8	+ 225.8	400.9	424.1	+ 23.2
United States.....	204.6	539.5	+ 334.9	334.1	916.8	+ 582.7
South America....	190.8	450.4	+ 259.6	329.5	575.0	+ 245.5
Other American countries[c].......	213.5	626.9	+ 413.4	271.9	333.7	+ 61.8
Total with outside areas.......	2,785.2	4,661.8	+1,876.6	3,852.3	5,219.4	+1,367.1
Trade between United Kingdom and Eire........	208.7	208.7	0.0	446.3	446.3	0.0
TOTAL........	2,993.9	4,870.5	+1,876.6	4,298.6	5,665.7	+1,367.1

II. WITH EMPIRE AND FOREIGN COUNTRIES

	Exports	Imports	Net[b]	Exports	Imports	Net[b]
British Empire countries.......	1,378.6	1,891.0	+ 512.4	1,909.2	1,669.2	− 240.0
Nazi Europe......	873.4	1,224.4	+ 351.0	1,205.1	1,826.3	+ 621.2
Other foreign countries...........	741.9	1,755.1	+1,013.2	1,184.3	2,170.2	+ 985.9
TOTAL........	2,993.9	4,870.5	+1,876.6	4,298.6	5,665.7	+1,367.1

[a] Sources of the data, and questions of method and definition, are considered in footnotes to the table on p. 147, and in App. A.
[b] Net imports (+), net exports (−).
[c] Other North America, Central America, and the West Indies.

All parts of the British Empire have some trade with Nazi Europe, but the British Isles alone account for most of the Empire total. In both years studied, the United Kingdom, together with Eire, accounted for roughly half of all Empire exports to Nazi Europe, and for three-fourths of the imports from there. Elsewhere in the Empire, India, Burma, and Ceylon had the largest

BRITISH EMPIRE TRADE WITH NAZI EUROPE AND THE WORLD, 1937, 1929[a]
(Dollar figures are in millions)
I. IN 1937

Empire Countries	Exports of Empire Countries		Imports of Empire Countries		Trade with Europe as Percentage of Total	
	To Europe	Total	From Europe	Total	Exports	Imports
United Kingdom....	$ 867.1	$2,883.7	$1,194.6	$ 4,655.4	30.1	25.7
Eire..............	6.3	110.2	29.8	215.1	5.7	13.9
British Isles, total.	$ 873.4	$2,993.9	$1,224.4	$ 4,870.5	29.2	25.1
Canada and Newfoundland........	$ 108.9	$1,145.8	$ 46.7	$ 832.3	9.5	5.6
Caribbean countries[b]	10.1	101.1	4.4	102.5	10.0	4.3
India, Burma, and Ceylon..........	255.3	1,098.0	123.4	648.6	23.3	19.0
Malay states.......	89.1	511.6	22.4	372.0	17.4	6.0
Other British Asia..	19.3	96.3	32.4	109.9	20.0	29.5
Oceania[c]..........	189.1	997.6	65.7	728.6	19.0	9.0
Union of South Africa.............	61.9	210.0	82.8	476.1	29.5	17.4
Other British Africa.	119.6	385.7	48.0	319.8	31.0	15.0
Total...........	$1,726.7	$7,540.0	$1,650.2	$ 8,460.3	22.9	19.5

II. IN 1929

	To Europe	Total	From Europe	Total	Exports	Imports
United Kingdom....	$1,199.8	$4,073.6	$1,804.1	$ 5,367.3	29.5	33.6
Eire..............	5.3	225.0	22.2	298.4	2.4	7.4
British Isles, total.	$1,205.1	$4,298.6	$1,826.3	$ 5,665.7	28.0	32.2
Canada and Newfoundland........	$ 229.5	$1,164.4	$ 94.9	$ 1,329.8	19.7	7.1
Caribbean countries[b]	30.1	104.0	5.6	101.0	28.9	5.5
India, Burma, and Ceylon..........	457.2	1,490.2	181.9	1,044.0	30.7	17.4
Malay states.......	23.0	451.7	34.5	488.3	5.1	7.1
Other British Asia..	6.7	71.9	16.2	74.9	9.3	21.6
Oceania[c]..........	259.7	971.6	106.1	952.8	26.7	11.1
Union of South Africa.............	94.5	212.7	72.9	404.2	44.4	18.0
Other British Africa.	98.7	312.5	55.9	312.1	31.6	17.9
Total...........	$2,404.5	$9,077.6	$2,394.3	$10,372.8	26.5	23.1

[a] Sources of the data are given in footnotes to the table on p. 147.
[b] British West Indies, British Honduras, and British Guiana.
[c] Trade of French possessions in Oceania is excluded where possible.

trade with the area; the Caribbean countries of the Empire had the smallest. The table on page 162 indicates the relative importance of Nazi Europe in the total trade of the several parts of the Empire.

As the table shows, trade with the Nazi area accounted for roughly one-fourth to one-fifth of the total trade of the Empire and for roughly one-third to one-fourth of the trade of the United Kingdom alone. For Eire, and for some British countries of the Western Hemisphere, including Canada, trade with the German area was small in comparison with the total.

For the area controlled by the Soviet Union, Nazi Europe is the principal market, and the principal source of supply. In fact, in 1929 exports to Europe were twice those to the British Isles, the market of second importance, while imports were three times those from the United States, the second largest source of imports. By 1937, the German area had lost considerable ground,

TRADE OF THE RUSSIAN AREA WITH OTHER WORLD AREAS, 1937, 1929[a]
(In millions of dollars)

Destination of Exports Source of Imports	1937			1929		
	Exports	Imports	Net[b]	Exports	Imports	Net[b]
Nazi Europe.......	377.3	322.3	− 55.0	505.2	488.9	− 16.3
British Isles........	320.4	115.6	−204.8	241.7	77.9	−163.8
Africa.............	15.7	12.1	− 3.6	15.3	14.4	− 0.9
Asia..............	41.1	79.0	+ 37.9	61.6	95.0	+ 33.4
Oceania...........	2.4	12.2	+ 9.8	1.3	12.4	+ 11.1
United States......	61.1	88.6	+ 27.5	41.6	144.7	+103.1
South America.....	11.5	25.8	+ 14.3	6.3	26.0	+ 19.7
Other American countries[c]........	1.4	19.7	+ 18.3	1.3	5.3	+ 4.0
All outside areas....	830.9	675.3	−155.6	874.3	864.6	− 9.7
Inter-country trade of the Russian area	27.3	27.3	0.0	48.8	48.8	0.0
Total	858.2	702.6	−155.6	923.1	913.4	− 9.7

[a] Sources of the data are given in footnotes to the table on p. 147.
[b] Net imports (+), net exports (−).
[c] Other North America, Central America, and the West Indies.

though it still ranked first in Russian-area trade. Trade with the British Isles had increased, putting Britain in second place as a source of Russian-area imports, and a very close second in the export trade.

Nazi Europe accounted for roughly 55 per cent of Russian-area trade in 1929, and for 45 per cent in 1937. In both years, Nazi Europe and Britain together took 81 per cent of the Russian-area exports, and supplied 62 per cent of the imports.

For the individual states, as for the whole Russian area, trade with Nazi Europe was very important. The table below shows Europe's position in this trade.

RUSSIAN-AREA TRADE WITH NAZI EUROPE AND THE WORLD, 1937, 1929[a]
(Dollar figures are in millions)

I. IN 1937

Russian Area	Russian-Area Exports		Russian-Area Imports		Trade with Europe as Percentage of Total	
	To Europe	Total	From Europe	Total	Exports	Imports
U.S.S.R.........	$150.4	$357.9	$ 98.2	$273.9	*42.0*	*35.9*
Estonia.........	15.4	31.5	14.1	27.6	*48.9*	*51.1*
Finland.........	87.6	243.0	108.8	202.5	*36.0*	*53.7*
Latvia..........	28.4	59.5	24.3	45.3	*47.7*	*53.6*
Lithuania.......	15.5	36.0	18.3	35.6	*43.1*	*51.4*
Half of Poland[b]..	80.0	130.3	58.6	117.7	*61.4*	*49.8*
Total.........	$377.3	$858.2	$322.3	$702.6	*44.0*	*45.9*

II. IN 1929

U.S.S.R.........	$222.3	$441.2	$170.8	$433.2	*50.4*	*39.4*
Estonia.........	13.5	29.4	17.8	32.6	*45.9*	*54.6*
Finland.........	84.5	183.3	116.5	174.1	*46.1*	*66.9*
Latvia..........	37.4	80.6	45.3	69.5	*46.4*	*65.2*
Lithuania.......	19.0	24.7	22.2	30.4	*76.9*	*73.0*
Half of Poland[b]..	128.5	163.9	116.3	173.6	*78.4*	*67.0*
Total.........	$505.2	$923.1	$488.9	$913.4	*54.7*	*53.5*

[a] Sources of the data are given in footnotes to the table on p. 147.

[b] An arbitrary distribution has been made of the trade of Poland and Dan-zig—half being put with the Russian area and half with Nazi Europe.

From 1929 to 1937, the German area lost ground in most parts of the Russian area, as well as in the group as a whole. But in every case Europe accounted for 36 per cent or more of the total, and in many cases the proportion was considerably more than 50 per cent.

More than half of Africa's growing volume of exports is shipped to the German area, and almost half of the imports come from there. The British Isles have stood second in this trade, although well below Nazi Europe. African exports to Britain in 1929 were less than half those to the German area, and considerably less than half in 1937. Imports from Britain were roughly 60 per cent of those from Europe. The United States—although accounting for only 8 per cent of African exports and 10 per cent of imports—ranked third in 1929; but by 1937 Asia had shifted to third place. Africa's trade

TRADE OF AFRICA WITH LARGE WORLD AREAS, 1937, 1929[a]
(In millions of dollars)

Destination of Exports Source of Imports	1937			1929		
	Exports	Imports	Net[b]	Exports	Imports	Net[b]
Nazi Europe.....	812.5	685.0	−127.5	692.8	733.4	+ 40.6
British Isles......	327.0	410.0	+ 83.0	334.6	424.0	+ 89.4
Russian area.....	12.1	15.7	+ 3.6	14.4	15.3	+ .9
Asia............	117.6	178.2	+ 60.6	66.2	125.9	+ 59.7
Oceania.........	3.7	5.3	+ 1.6	5.3	21.8	+ 16.5
United States....	92.0	160.7	+ 68.7	108.0	155.6	+ 47.6
South America...	3.0	17.9	+ 14.9	.2	24.2	+ 24.0
Other American countries[c]......	15.6	31.4	+ 15.8	4.3	19.5	+ 15.2
All outside areas..	1,383.5	1,504.2	+120.7	1,225.8	1,519.7	+293.9
Inter-country trade of Africa..	80.8	80.8	0.0	105.7	105.7	0.0
Total	1,464.3	1,585.0	+120.7	1,331.5	1,625.4	+293.9

[a] Sources of the data, and questions of method and definition, are considered in footnotes to the table on p. 147 and in App. A.
[b] Net imports (+), net exports (−).
[c] Other North America, Central America, and the West Indies.

with other world regions was of very small proportions, both in absolute and relative terms.

Most of the countries of Africa have extraordinarily close trade connections with the German area. The exceptions are Liberia and British-controlled countries and territories. In general, of course, the colonial status of the continent affords the principal explanation of exist-

TRADE OF AFRICAN COUNTRIES WITH NAZI
(Dollar figures

I. IN 1937

Africa	Exports from Africa		Imports to Africa		Trade with Europe as Percentage of Total	
	To Europe	Total	From Europe	Total	Ex-ports	Im-ports
Mediterranean Africa:						
Algeria................	$164.4	$ 189.1	$135.3	$ 158.2	*86.9*	*85.5*
French and Spanish						
Morocco..........	54.5	72.8	46.2	75.7	*74.9*	*61.0*
Tunisia..............	38.9	53.7	40.0	49.5	*72.4*	*80.8*
Egypt..............	94.6	229.7	92.8	192.5	*41.2*	*48.2*
Libya..............	4.8	5.7	29.5	31.9	*84.2*	*92.5*
Total.............	$357.2	$ 551.0	$343.8	$ 507.8	*64.8*	*67.7*
British controlled:						
Union of S. Africa	$ 61.9	$ 210.0	$ 82.8	$ 476.1	*29.5*	*17.4*
Other..............	119.6	385.7	48.0	319.8	*31.0*	*15.0*
Total.............	$181.5	$ 595.7	$130.8	$ 795.9	*30.5*	*16.4*
French controlled (excluding Mediterranean).............	$126.3	$ 138.8	$ 61.4	$ 86.8	*91.0*	*70.7*
Italian controlled (excluding Libya)...	13.2	17.1	114.3	126.4	*77.2*	*90.4*
Belgian colonies.......	88.6	96.2	19.5	38.2	*92.1*	*51.0*
Portuguese colonies....	27.6	45.0	14.7	28.0	*61.3*	*52.5*
Liberia..............	1.2	2.4	.5	1.9	*50.0*	*26.3*
Country not specified...	16.9	18.1	—	—	*93.4*	—
All Africa..........	$812.5	$1,464.3	$685.0	$1,585.0	*55.5*	*43.2*

ᵃ Compiled from sources cited in footnote to table, p. 147.

ing trade ties. The preponderant importance of Nazi Europe in the trade of many political divisions of Africa, and its relatively minor place in some countries, is indicated by the accompanying table.

The figures for 1937 show that in Mediterranean Africa, taken as a whole, roughly two-thirds of the trade was with Europe. If Egypt, with its British ties,

EUROPE AND THE WORLD, 1937, 1929[a]
are in millions)

II. IN 1929

Africa	Exports from Africa		Imports to Africa		Trade with Europe as Percentage of Total	
	To Europe	Total	From Europe	Total	Exports	Imports
Mediterranean Africa:						
Algeria............	$135.2	$ 166.1	$192.1	$ 228.8	*81.4*	*84.0*
French and Spanish						
Morocco.........	49.5	63.6	71.1	98.5	*77.8*	*72.2*
Tunisia...........	37.1	49.1	60.7	76.9	*75.6*	*78.9*
Egypt............	110.1	305.1	126.8	279.2	*36.1*	*45.4*
Libya............	4.2	5.5	13.9	17.8	*76.4*	*78.1*
Total...........	$336.1	$ 589.4	$464.6	$ 701.2	*57.0*	*66.3*
British controlled:						
Union of S. Africa	$ 94.5	$ 212.7	$ 72.9	$ 404.2	*44.4*	*18.0*
Other............	98.7	312.5	55.9	312.1	*31.6*	*17.9*
Total...........	$193.2	$ 525.2	$128.8	$ 716.3	*36.8*	*18.0*
French controlled (excluding Mediterranean)...........	$ 83.0	$ 97.2	$ 77.6	$ 100.4	*85.4*	*77.3*
Italian controlled (excluding Libya)...	5.0	16.3	7.3	14.7	*30.7*	*49.7*
Belgian colonies......	52.2	64.4	36.4	55.5	*81.1*	*65.6*
Portuguese colonies....	19.6	32.0	18.3	35.9	*61.3*	*51.0*
Liberia.............	.6	.9	.4	1.4	*66.7*	*28.6*
Country not specified...	3.1	6.1	—	—	*50.8*	—
All Africa..........	$692.8	$1,331.5	$733.4	$1,625.4	*52.0*	*45.1*

is excluded from the reckoning, the ratio is approximately 80 per cent. In the case of the important French colony of Algeria, and for Italian-controlled Libya, the ratio is even higher. For some of the colonial groups farther south, as much as 90 per cent of their export or import trade was with Europe. For Liberia and for British Empire countries, the trade was much less important. Even with these included, however, it will be seen that in 1929, as well as in 1937, European markets took well over 50 per cent of all African exports, and supplied something like 45 per cent of total imports.

Nazi Europe and the United States are of almost equal importance in the trade of Asia. The distribution of the trade among large world areas in 1937 and 1929 is shown by the accompanying table.

TRADE OF ASIA WITH LARGE WORLD AREAS, 1937, 1929[a]
(In millions of dollars)

Destination of Exports Source of Imports	1937			1929		
	Exports	Imports	Net[b]	Exports	Imports	Net[b]
Nazi Europe.....	954.8	642.3	−312.5	1,057.5	812.2	−245.3
British Isles......	622.4	452.3	−170.1	567.2	808.9	+241.7
Russian area.....	79.0	41.1	− 37.9	95.0	61.6	− 33.4
Africa...........	178.2	117.6	− 60.6	125.9	66.2	− 59.7
Oceania.........	130.4	106.9	− 23.5	131.0	138.5	+ 7.5
United States....	968.9	642.2	−326.7	1,278.9	744.7	−534.2
South America...	78.4	49.5	− 28.9	56.8	7.2	− 49.6
Other American countries[c]......	76.4	55.4	− 21.0	61.9	76.7	+ 14.8
All outside areas..	3,088.5	2,107.3	−981.2	3,374.2	2,716.0	−658.2
Inter-country trade of Asia...	1,532.4	1,532.4	0.0	1,861.9	1,861.9	0.0
Total..........	4,620.9	3,639.7	−981.2	5,236.1	4,577.9	−658.2

[a] Sources of the data, and questions of method and definition, are considered in footnotes to the table on p. 147 and in App. A.

[b] Net imports (+), net exports (−).

[c] Other North America, Central America, and the West Indies.

In the export trade, the United States stood first in both years considered here. Nazi Europe stood first in the import trade, though the margin was very narrow in 1937. However, trade with both of these outside areas, taken together, scarcely equalled the inter-country trade of the Orient—which represented about 33 to 35 per cent of total exports, and 40 to 42 per cent of total imports.

The countries of Australasia differ widely as regards their trade with Nazi Europe. Some of them have also shown considerable shifts in the direction of their trade in recent years. Iraq, for example, sent less than 5 per cent of her exports to Europe in 1929 but more than 54 per cent in 1937 when the recently completed pipeline was delivering oil from her newly developed fields. Meantime there was a relative increase in Malayan exports to Nazi Europe, and a marked decrease in those from Australia. The way in which the political divisions of Asia and Oceania divided their trade between Europe and the rest of the world in 1929 and 1937 is shown by the table on page 170.

In general, the German area was less important in the trade of the independent and British-controlled countries of Asia and was a major factor in the case of the French colonies. Japan, for example, sent less than 6 per cent of her exports to Europe in 1937 and brought less than 10 per cent of her imports from there. At the same time, Europe accounted for 55 per cent of the foreign trade of French Indo-China and other French colonies in Asia outside the Mediterranean area.

For all countries of Asia and Oceania combined, roughly one-fifth of the export trade and one-sixth of the import trade were with countries now under German control—both in 1929 and 1937.

I. in 1937

Asia and Oceania	Australasian Exports		Australasian Imports		Trade with Europe as Percentage of Total	
	To Europe	Total	From Europe	Total	Ex-ports	Im-ports
Mediterranean Asia:						
Turkey............	$ 70.2	$ 108.7	$ 57.0	$ 91.5	64.6	62.3
Syria and Lebanon..	6.9	22.8	19.3	39.8	30.3	48.5
Palestine..........	8.5	29.9	29.4	66.2	28.4	44.4
Cyprus............	1.1	7.2	2.7	8.5	15.3	31.8
Total............	$ 86.7	$ 168.6	$108.4	$ 206.0	51.4	52.6
Arabia[b].............	$ 2.5	$ 17.7	—	$ 22.2	14.1	—
Iraq................	48.2	88.4	$ 6.9	40.9	54.5	16.9
Iran................	37.3	151.1	17.1	52.2	24.7	32.8
Total............	$ 88.0	$ 257.2	$ 24.0	$ 115.3	34.2	20.8
British controlled (not given above)						
India and Burma[c]...	$ 243.8	$ 982.9	$116.8	$ 560.0	24.8	20.9
Malay states.......	89.1	511.6	22.4	372.0	17.4	6.0
Ceylon............	11.5	115.1	6.6	88.6	10.0	7.4
All other[d].........	7.2	41.5	.3	13.0	17.3	2.3
Total............	$ 351.6	$1,651.1	$146.1	$1,033.6	21.3	14.1
French controlled (not given above)[e]......	$ 72.5	$ 130.8	$ 36.4	$ 65.7	55.4	55.4
Dutch East Indies....	173.4	625.7	97.5	269.4	27.7	36.2
Japanese Empire[f].....	54.2	990.3	108.3	1,137.2	5.5	9.5
Manchukuo and Kwan-tung..............	37.2	157.3	11.0	255.3	23.6	4.3
China and Hong Kong[g]	80.0	392.0	92.7	397.8	20.4	23.3
Siam................	4.7	89.1	7.1	50.5	5.3	14.1
Philippine Islands.....	6.5	158.8	10.8	108.9	4.1	9.9
Total Asia.......	$ 954.8	$4,620.9	$642.3	$3,639.7	20.7	17.6
Australia............	$ 161.6	$ 684.6	$ 52.7	$ 497.5	23.6	10.6
New Zealand.........	16.6	288.0	13.0	222.8	5.8	5.8
Other Oceania........	10.9	25.0	1.9	11.5	43.6	16.5
Total Oceania....	$ 189.1	$ 997.6	$ 67.6	$ 731.8	19.0	9.2
Asia and Oceania.....	$1,143.9	$5,618.5	$709.9	$4,371.5	20.4	16.2

[a] Compiled from sources cited in footnote a to table, p. 147.
[b] Mainly Aden (British), but includes other countries in the peninsula.
[c] Excludes trade between India and Burma.
[d] Mainly British Borneo, Sarawak, etc., but may include some non-British.

EUROPE, AND THE WORLD, 1937, 1929[a]
are in millions)

II. IN 1929

Asia and Oceania	Australasian Exports		Australasian Imports		Trade with Europe as Percentage of Total	
	To Europe	Total	From Europe	Total	Ex-ports	Im-ports
Mediterranean Asia:						
Turkey.............	$ 53.7	$ 96.2	$ 78.4	$ 123.4	55.8	63.5
Syria and Lebanon..	4.9	22.7	24.6	53.5	21.6	46.0
Palestine..........	1.9	12.4	10.9	32.2	15.3	33.9
Cyprus............	1.6	4.8	3.9	9.2	33.3	42.4
Total............	$ 62.1	$ 136.1	$117.8	$ 218.3	45.6	54.0
Arabia[b]..............	$ 1.6	$ 16.4	$ 1.1	$ 22.7	9.8	4.8
Iraq................	1.1	26.5	9.9	35.5	4.2	27.9
Iran................	35.9	142.6	15.2	72.9	25.2	20.9
Total............	$ 38.6	$ 185.5	$ 26.2	$ 131.1	20.8	20.0
British controlled (not given above)						
India and Burma[c]...	$ 447.7	$1,353.5	$169.6	$ 897.3	33.1	18.9
Malay states.......	23.0	451.7	34.5	488.3	5.1	7.1
Ceylon............	9.5	136.7	12.3	146.7	6.9	8.4
All other[d].........	1.6	38.3	.3	10.8	4.2	2.8
Total............	$ 481.8	$1,980.2	$216.7	$1,543.1	24.3	14.0
French controlled (not given above)[e].....	$ 29.2	$ 120.1	$ 52.1	$ 97.8	24.3	53.3
Dutch East Indies....	201.8	733.4	148.6	418.7	27.5	35.5
Japanese Empire[f]...,.	40.0	1,013.0	124.7	1,087.6	3.9	11.5
Manchukuo and Kwan-tung............	—	—	—	—	—	—
China and Hong Kong[g]	179.2	797.7	99.4	844.5	22.5	11.8
Siam................	3.5	100.7	14.5	89.5	3.5	16.2
Philippine Islands.....	21.3	169.4	12.2	147.3	12.6	8.3
Total Asia.......	$1,057.5	$5,236.1	$812.2	$4,577.9	20.2	17.7
Australia............	$ 244.8	$ 694.9	$ 87.3	$ 707.4	35.2	12.3
New Zealand.........	11.3	257.2	18.8	236.6	4.4	7.9
Other Oceania........	7.0	25.9	4.6	14.4	27.0	31.9
Total Oceania....	$ 263.1	$ 978.0	$110.7	$ 958.4	26.9	11.6
Asia and Oceania.....	$1,320.6	$6,214.1	$922.9	$5,536.3	21.3	16.7

[e] French Indo-China and French establishments in India.

[f] Includes Japan, Chosen, and Taiwan but excludes intra-Empire trade.

[g] Excludes the trade between China and Hong Kong; in 1929 includes Manchukuo. On 1929 figure for Hong Kong trade see note o, p. 191.

SUMMARY

The foregoing pages have presented a survey of the geographic distribution of Nazi Europe's trade. To summarize what has already been said, the accompanying table and map show the trade of this area with all other large world areas. They also give a general view of the relative importance of this trade to all of the areas taking part in it. In addition, the table shows how the trade of the whole world was divided among the several large areas.

WORLD TRADE IN RELATION TO NAZI EUROPE, 1937, 1929

World Areas	Exports				Imports			
	Total (In millions of dollars)		Percentage of Total Sent to Nazi Europe		Total (In millions of dollars)		Percentage of Total Taken from Nazi Europe	
	1937	1929	1937	1929	1937	1929	1937	1929
British Isles..........	2,994	4,299	29	28	4,870	5,666	25	32
Russian area.........	858	923	44	55	703	913	46	54
Africa...............	1,464	1,331	56	52	1,585	1,625	43	45
Asia.................	4,621	5,236	21	20	3,640	4,578	18	18
Oceania.............	998	978	19	27	732	958	9	12
United States........	3,408	5,654	23	28	3,081	4,396	19	22
South America.......	2,083	2,606	39	38	1,241	1,870	36	35
Other Western Hemisphere..............	1,894	2,014	16	21	1,497	2,117	10	11
All countries outside Nazi Europe.......	18,320	23,041	28	29	17,349	22,123	24	26
Nazi Europe[a]........	8,637	12,072	52	52	9,608	12.990	47	48
WORLD TOTAL[a].......	26,957	35,113	36	37	26,957	35,113	32	34

[a] The intra-area exports of Nazi Europe (included in both these totals) amounted to 4,516 million dollars in 1937, and 6,266 million in 1929. The total for intra-area imports, of course, exactly equals that for exports.

Trade with Europe was of greater relative importance to the Russian-controlled states and Africa than to any other large world area, and also accounted for well over a third of South American exports and imports. In absolute amounts, however, Europe's trade with the British Isles was of outstanding importance.

More than half of Nazi Europe's exports went to other countries in the area, and almost half of its larger volume of imports was also intra-area in character. With this trade included, exports to Nazi Europe make up more than one-third of total world exports, while imports from Europe make up almost one-third of the world total. But a comparison on this basis overstates the importance of Europe's trade in relation to the rest of the world. As the table shows, less than 30 per cent of total exports from countries *outside* the area were shipped to Nazi Europe in both years studied, and roughly 25 per cent of the imports of outside countries were taken from the states now under German control.

Shifts in the direction of trade are indicated by the percentage comparisons given in the table. Roughly 55 per cent of Russian-area trade was with Nazi Europe in 1929, compared with 44 per cent in 1937. During the eight-year period covered by the table, Britain reduced both the absolute and relative amounts she imported from Europe—in favor of trade with Empire countries. Oceania, the United States, and the "other Western Hemisphere" group sold a much smaller proportion of their exports in Nazi Europe in 1937 than in 1929—largely as a result of the efforts various European countries were making to bring their commodity imports into balance with their exports.

CONCLUSIONS

The foregoing survey of Nazi Europe's trade and production—although it covers years that are past and conditions that no longer exist—was not made for its bearing on the past. On the contrary, its primary purpose is to throw light on the future. We have not undertaken to forecast the outcome of the present conflict in Europe, nor its effects on the future political organization and administration of the area. What we have done is to weigh the area's resources against its requirements in two reasonably favorable past years, and thereby gauge some of the important elements of strength and weakness in its future economic position. The inherent advantages and handicaps revealed by past experience will remain, whether the political organization and administration of the area are such as to promote or to obstruct full utilization of its resources. Moreover, these factors promise to play an important part in determining the future trade of the area, including trade with Western Hemisphere countries.

The factual data which have been presented could be interpreted in terms of any one of several hypotheses as to the future political organization of the world. Because of widespread concern over the potentiality of a German-dominated continent of Europe, the hypothesis upon which our study was focused was that of German control over the whole of continental Europe except Russia and the states in the Russian sphere.[1] All other countries were treated as foreign territory. This means that the resources and trade of the colonial possessions

[1] For the purposes of the analysis at various points, we have also considered the probable effect of including in the area the countries bordering the Mediterranean on the south.

of countries now occupied by Germany were left outside
the reckoning, but account was taken in Chapter V of
the returns they pay to Europeans. It was also assumed
that there will be a consolidation and utilization for the
whole area of the sources of international income that
formerly supplied foreign purchasing power for the separate countries of the area.

No attempt was made to evaluate losses in productive
capacity caused by the destruction and dislocation now
in progress, nor the increased output that may result
from future improvements in production techniques.
Likewise, no question was raised concerning possible
changes in standards of living in Europe, and changes
in import requirements that might follow. In short, it
was assumed that after the war the area will return to
the levels of production and consumption prevailing in
1929, or at least to those of 1937.

Starting with this general hypothesis, consideration
has been given to the trade problem as it might concern
the Nazi government, if it were left in control of the area
at the end of the war. And from this, certain conclusions
have been reached with regard to the basic difficulties
affecting the area's trade with the rest of the world, and
certain suggestions made concerning possible future
changes in the area's international economic position.

*Nazi Europe, taken as a whole, has been a net importer
of food and raw materials.* And unless conditions are very
different from those we have assumed, it will continue
to import both classes of commodities in large amounts.
Its climate, soil, and topography, and the poverty of its
subsoil, all place limitations on its domestic output.
Even assuming that, with a better organization of productive resources, its agricultural output might be increased and its mineral deposits used more effectively,

many commodities still would have to be imported from outside sources.

Without imports of food (and feedstuffs), Nazi Europe's population would go on short rations. Their diet would not only become much more monotonous than it has been in the past, but there probably would be a shortage of cereals, and a very serious shortage of fats. Consumption of vegetable oils would have to be reduced —probably by as much as 50 per cent. Consumption of fats in the form of meat and dairy products would also have to be considerably reduced, owing to the shortage of feedstuffs.

Without imported raw materials from fields and forests outside the area, the wheels of industry would turn very slowly. Practically nothing would remain of the great textile industries of the area—with cotton and wool spinning and weaving practically at a standstill, the silk supply reduced by about 40 per cent, no jute available, and even the use of flax and hemp considerably curtailed. Some expansion in the use of woodpulp for the manufacture of artificial fibers would be possible, but would fall far short of supplying enough to turn the spindles and looms formerly employed in the manufacture of natural fibers. Leather-working industries would be slowed down considerably. Rubber would have to be supplied entirely from synthetic sources, and this in turn would create additional raw-material problems.

Without imports of industrial minerals, the area's manufacturing, mining, transportation, communication, and even agriculture would be severely handicapped. Of outstanding importance would be the lack of modern machines and machine tools, whose manufacture could not be continued. The strategic factor here would be the area's deficiency in most of the important alloy metals, notwithstanding its adequate supply of iron ore and its excess steel capacity. There would also be a shortage of bearing metals for machines with movable parts. The automotive industries would also lack asbestos for brake linings, mica for spark plugs, and to a considerable extent would be dependent on motor fuels from synthetic sources. The electrical industries and those dependent on them would be hampered by a shortage of copper— and of many other minerals that are used in smaller amounts. And, while aluminum might replace copper, this would require a considerable increase in the area's production of aluminum. The printing and publishing industries would lack good type metal.

In coal, Nazi Europe probably would be able to supply its own requirements, convenience of transportation from Britain to the countries deficient in coal being the principal explanation for net imports into the area in the past. However, resort to synthetic methods of production—in the case of rubber, "silk" hose, and gasoline, for example—might result in a shortage of coal in the future. In a few other minerals, such as nitrate, potash, gypsum, and sulphur, the area has abundant resources. In mercury, it is practically in a monopoly position.

The area's net imports of food and raw materials have been considerably larger than its net exports of manufactures. In fact, imports of all classes of commodities exceeded exports by 1.6 billion dollars in 1929, and by 1.3 billions in 1937. Meantime, the old Reich had small net exports of commodities in both years. The figures below, in millions of dollars, show how the trade of old Germany has compared with that of Nazi Europe.

	Germany (Old boundaries)		Nazi Europe (Including Germany)	
1937:				
Food, net imports..........	607.4		648.2	
Raw materials, net imports..	931.4	1,538.8	2,594.7	3,242.9
Manufactures, net exports...		1,716.7		1,941.0
Total—Net exports.......		177.9		—
Net imports.......		—		1,301.9
1929:				
Food, net imports..........	773.6		949.5	
Raw materials, net imports...	1,018.8	1,792.4	3,213.5	4,163.0
Manufactures, net exports...		1,800.9		2,554.6
Total—Net exports.......		8.5		—
Net imports.......		—		1,608.4

As the table shows, Germany's supply problem has not been solved by her seizure of neighboring territories. On the contrary, it has been made more difficult. Raw-material imports, in particular, are considerably larger for the whole area than they were for Germany alone— whether they are measured in absolute or in relative terms.

Increased territorial specialization is sometimes proposed as a way of meeting existing shortages in foods and raw materials, thereby solving the trade problem. For example, German sources indicate that in the future, Germany proper—with perhaps a few other industrial countries of Europe—will specialize in manufacturing, while other countries of the Nazi area will make every effort to increase their "primary" production. In this way they expect to ensure better machinery and better production methods for agriculture, with a resulting increase in agricultural output. They also expect that the proposed centralization and co-ordination of manufactures will lead to a more effective utilization of plant, and of the special skills of industrial workers.

A consideration of problems concerned with the production and use of materials and the way these may be affected by increased territorial specialization and by the application of new inventions and technologies lies outside the scope of this investigation. However, it is clear that Europe will have to depend on trade for necessary supplies of many important commodities. For example, rubber, palm kernels, coffee, and cotton cannot now—and probably cannot in the future—be economically grown in Europe. Nor can tin, copper, chromite, and various other minerals be mined, in the quantities needed, since the ores for these metals are entirely lacking in the area's subsoil, or are found in inadequate amounts. And if these commodities are supplied by trade, the problem of providing payment for them will have to be faced.

The large gap between the commodity imports and exports of the area has been bridged by international receipts from many sources. In the main, these have come from the tourist trade, from emigrant remittances, from shipping earnings, insurance, and commissions. The net total of interest and dividends for the whole area was not large, probably adding something to the payments that had to be made in 1929, for example, and providing some additional means of payment in 1937. In some past years, receipts from all of these sources have fallen short of meeting payments on imports, and the account has been balanced by borrowing—principally in the United States and Great Britain.

If the tourist trade, receipts from emigrants, and other so-called service "trades" continue to yield as large an income for the area in the future as in the past, and if exports can be maintained at the 1937 levels, it would seem that, in the main, future import require-ments can be met without large new borrowing from outside countries. (In saying this, as we have pointed out above, we are not taking account of postwar reconstruction of devastated areas.) This would mean that the investment funds of the more prosperous states of the area would have to be made available to some of the other states in need of funds. It would also mean that these more prosperous states would have smaller amounts than formerly for investment in outside areas —for example, in the colonies, and in the United States. It is an open question, however, whether the area's future international income will be maintained at the levels of former years.

A Nazi regime for Europe might involve some decline in its service income. If Paris, for example, is no longer the gay capital of a free French nation, it may no longer attract the dollars of foreign students, or of pleasure-seeking or sentimental tourists. And if the wholesale disorganization and destruction in Europe weakens the ties of affection which account for emigrant remittances from all parts of the world, receipts from this source may be considerably diminished. Adverse effects on shipping earnings appear less probable.

What may happen to European receipts of interest and dividends from abroad is also a matter for speculation. At present the United States and Great Britain are not permitting the withdrawal of investments owned in countries invaded by the Germans. And in the event that the invasion is followed by permanent occupation, it is not impossible that such investments might be liquidated by some kind of international claims commission, and the funds used to offset American and British investments of various kinds in Europe. Moreover, if Japan should succeed in extending control in the Pacific, receipts from French and Dutch investments there might also be considerably reduced. Altogether, the prospect would seem to be for some shrinkage in income from services.

A shrinkage in receipts from services (or borrowing) would necessitate changes in the area's commodity trade. Either imports would have to be reduced or exports expanded. But raw-material imports are required for the production of manufactured exports. Therefore, it would be difficult to cut imports without cutting exports, or to expand exports without expanding imports.[2] If the choice lay with the Nazi area, a real dilemma would face those responsible for decisions regarding trade policies. But a serious shrinkage in service income might be in itself a decisive factor in determining the area's future position in world trade. This possibility is frequently overlooked.

It is often assumed that at the close of present hostilities Nazi Europe will be in an advantageous position in its trade with the rest of the world because everywhere, except in Great Britain, its commodity imports are in excess of its exports. That is, everywhere except in Britain it buys more than it sells[3] and, therefore, it stands in the position of a "good customer" in all parts of the world except Britain. Because of this fact, it is argued, Nazi Europe will be able to get preferred treatment for the goods it will offer for sale in those markets, and will be able to crowd out competing products from other exporting countries.

In this argument, no allowance is made for the pos-

---

[2] The character of the area's principal exports of manufactured goods is indicated by the table in App. B.

[3] An outstanding example of a country dependent on Nazi Europe as a large market for its exports was Argentina—which formerly sold there half of its total exports of hides and skins, half of its wool exports, half of its grain exports, and a large part of its linseed crop.

sible future reduction in the area's capacity to pay for the excess imports it requires, and the effect this would have on exports. In fact, without any direct reference to the area's service income, it is tacitly assumed that such income will not decline, and that Europe will be able to continue its former large purchases of goods from external sources. However, when account *is* taken of the possible future loss of tourist income, income from emigrant remittances, and perhaps a reduction in interest and dividends from outside sources, the outlook is less optimistic.

A good customer is a good customer only so long as there is a prospect that he will be able to meet his bills. But if he lacks means of payment, and if his credit standing is impaired, he is not likely to continue in a preferred position. In the case of Nazi Europe, a reduction in service income probably would mean that commodity purchases in foreign markets would have to be reduced, and this in turn would probably lead to a reduction in exports. To some extent, perhaps, this decline in exports would follow because the area would no longer enjoy its former advantage as a large buyer. But even more important is the fact—indicated above—that in the main the goods that Nazi Europe ships to outside markets are manufactured goods that are made in whole or in part from imported raw materials.

A change in British policy might conceivably result in a considerable shrinkage in Nazi Europe's exports. In the past, exports to the British Isles have provided a very substantial supply of the foreign exchange used by Nazi Europe in the purchase of imports from other areas. If Britain should divert a considerable fraction of this trade to other sources of supply, this would seriously impair the German area's exporting and paying capacity. It would also help to readjust trade relations in other parts of the world.

It should be noted, of course, that such a shift would involve some changes in the character of British consumption habits—or in the character of exports from the new sources of supply. Dairy products and bacon will serve as examples. It would not be difficult for producers in North and South America to supply the British market with butter and cheese that would compete in quality with the Danish and Dutch products. They could also readily furnish bacon in quantities sufficient to supplant the Danish variety—but not of the quality wanted in the British market. Hogs raised on corn grown in the Argentine, and particularly those fed on the Corn Belt farms of the United States, yield a much fatter type of bacon than that which Britain has been in the habit of buying from Denmark. It is possible, however, that some changes might be made in breeds and in the methods used in fattening, slaughtering, and curing pork products in the Americas, with a view to meeting the British taste. Also, British consumers might make some concessions in favor of American producers. Shifts such as these would directly affect Nazi Europe's purchasing power in external markets.

The difficulties involved in the export-import problem of the future promise that Nazi Europe will probably impose a comprehensive system of controls over its external trade. And, if the trade of the whole area should be placed under the direction of a central organization, no doubt hard bargains could be forced upon unorganized groups of producers in outside countries. Germany has already experimented with such controls and put them in force, and probably would undertake to fit her system to the needs of the larger area. That such an effort would be met by counter-organization in other countries goes without saying. However, it is not the purpose of this book to consider the nature of the trade war that may eventuate following the end of the present conflict in Europe. One purpose has been to point out some of the limitations under which the trade and production of the area will have to operate in the future.

Undoubtedly, Europe's threatened trade war could prove a major world disturbance. This is indicated by the intricate web of trade connections that have linked together the economies of countries in Europe and in outside areas. However, the import requirements of Nazi Europe are so large and so varied that she is scarcely in a position to buy or refrain from buying at will. Her exports are wanted, but are not indispensable. Barring the use of force, her position in world markets will be as weak or as strong as her capacity to pay for the goods she needs. Clearly this is an issue whose outcome cannot be dictated entirely by Nazi Europe.

APPENDIXES

TRADE AREAS AND THE DIRECTION OF TRADE

In Chapter VI, statistics for *exports* as well as for imports were compiled from the official *import* data of the importing countries. In this way world exports for each of the years studied were made exactly equal to world imports. This would not have been the case if the export figures had been compiled from *reported exports*. On the latter basis, world exports are usually about 7 per cent smaller than world imports, the difference in 1937 amounting to roughly 2.2 billion dollars. This is because most countries include ocean transportation and insurance in the value of their imports but not in their exports.[1]

In general, the use of import statistics by country of origin (or country of consignment where origin is not shown), accomplishes two purposes: (1) It puts imports and exports on a comparable basis so far as the inclusion of insurance and freight charges are concerned. (2) With some few exceptions, it gives a truer picture of the destination of exports—for, as everyone knows who is familiar with the peculiarities of official trade data, probably the most unreliable of all are those purporting to show the destination of exports. In fact, goods are often shipped subject to a change of sailing orders at some later port of call, so that even the exporter may

---

[1] There are some exceptions, however. The following countries exclude ocean transportation and insurance from import values as well as export: Canada, Mexico, Cuba, certain Central American countries, the Philippine Islands, the Union of South Africa, and the United States.

not know the destination of his goods at the time they leave port. The source of imports, on the contrary, is ordinarily determined with less difficulty—although some countries show country of *shipment* rather than country of *origin* in their official reports.

In the case of certain countries, especially those having a large transit or re-export trade, the figures for exports, as compiled from the import data of other countries, may be considerably greater, or even smaller, than the officially reported exports.

Other factors also account for some of the difference between the figures as we have given them in Chapter VI and those given in official trade reports. Among these are: (1) There is a time lag between the shipment and receipt of goods. (2) The rules covering the recording of trade by customhouse officials vary from country to country. (3) Some countries group a portion of their imports, with the country of origin (or consignment) "not specified." Obviously, it was necessary to exclude such imports, and exports, from the analysis of Chapter VI. (4) A few small trade areas were omitted from the analysis, for example, Greenland, Iceland, Malta, and Nepal. (5) Some discrepancies between the export figures compiled from imports and exports as officially reported defy explanation. For example, total reported exports from Spanish Morocco amounted to only $1,900,000 in 1937, while Germany alone reported imports of iron ore from Spanish Morocco valued at $6,400,000 (or 1,071,080 metric tons of ore).

In the table below the trade figures given in Chapter VI are compared with the official trade figures for the principal countries or groups of countries in the world. Where small areas have been grouped together in the table, the component territories are shown by footnotes to the table.

DATA FROM CHAPTER VI COMPARED WITH OFFICIAL TRADE FIGURES, 1937[a]

(In millions of United States dollars, at current rates of exchange)

Country	Chapter VI		Officially Reported	
	Imports	Exports	Imports	Exports
NAZI EUROPE:				
Albania............................	6	4	6	3
Austria.............................	272	232	273	228
Belgium-Luxemburg.................	918	876	920	857
Bulgaria............................	63	60	63	65
Czechoslovakia.....................	382	389	383	419
Denmark...........................	367	340	369	355
France.............................	1,698	1,003	1,700	956
Germany...........................	2,182	2,300	2,199	2,376
Greece.............................	137	94	138	87
Hungary............................	140	165	140	173
Italy...............................	726	571	728	549
Netherlands........................	849	705	853	632
Norway............................	317	232	321	205
Half of Poland and Danzig...........	118	130	119	113
Portugal............................	97	90	105	54
Rumania...........................	148	276	148	230
Spain..............................	121	170	[b][121]	[b][170]
Sweden............................	534	556	541	510
Switzerland........................	413	279	413	295
Yugoslavia.........................	120	167	121	145
Total.........................	9,608	8,639	9,661	8,422
BRITISH ISLES:				
Eire...............................	215	110	218	110
United Kingdom....................	4,655	2,884	4,716	2,579
Total.........................	4,870	2,994	4,934	2,689
RUSSIAN AREA:				
Estonia............................	28	32	30	29

[a] The figures for Chapter VI were compiled from U. S. Dept. of Commerce, *Foreign Commerce Yearbook*, 1938, and for 1929 from *Commerce Yearbook*, Vol. II, 1930, 1931, supplemented by the official trade reports of all political subdivisions of the world. The officially reported figures are from official trade reports or from a secondary source such as U. S. Dept. of Commerce, *Foreign Commerce Yearbook*, 1938, or League of Nations, *Review of World Trade*, 1938. Excludes trade in gold and in coins wherever possible. The data are for calendar years except for Newfoundland, Haiti, Honduras, Burma, Aden, Iraq, Iran, Siam, New Guinea, and Papua.

[b] Spain did not publish any official trade report in 1937. These figures, like those in the preceding columns, were compiled from the reports of countries trading with Spain.

DATA FROM CHAPTER VI COMPARED WITH OFFICIAL TRADE
FIGURES, 1937[a]—*Continued*

Country	Chapter VI		Officially Reported	
	Imports	Exports	Imports	Exports
Finland............................	203	243	203	205
Latvia.............................	45	60	45	51
Lithuania..........................	36	36	36	35
Half of Poland and Danzig..........	118	130	119	113
U.S.S.R...........................	274	358	275	346
Total...........................	704	859	708	779
AFRICA:				
Mediterranean Area:				
Algeria..........................	158	189	166	173
Egypt............................	193	230	193	196
French and Spanish Morocco.......	76	73	77	48
Libya............................	32	6	33	6
Tunisia..........................	50	54	54	46
British controlled:				
Union of South Africa.............	476	210	476	188
Other[c]..........................	320	386	345	367
French controlled (excluding Mediterranean)[d]........................	87	139	117	116
Italian East Africa[e]................	126	17	130	18
Belgian colonies[f]..................	38	96	42	88
Portuguese colonies[g]...............	28	45	29	31
Liberia...........................	2	2	2	2
Country not specified..............	—	18	[h]	[h]
Total Africa.....................	1,586	1,465	1,664	1,279
ASIA:				
Mediterranean Asia:				
Cyprus..........................	9	7	11	10
Palestine........................	66	30	79	29

[c] Comprises Anglo-Egyptian Sudan, British Cameroons, Gambia, Gold Coast, Kenya and Uganda, Mauritius, Nigeria, Northern Rhodesia, Nyasaland Protectorate, Seychelles Islands, Somaliland Protectorate, Sierra Leone, Southern Rhodesia, St. Helena, Tanganyika, Territory of Southwest Africa, British Togo, and Zanzibar Protectorate.

[d] Comprises French Cameroon, French Equatorial Africa, Madagascar, Reunion, French Somaliland, French Togo, and French West Africa.

[e] Comprises Ethiopia, Eritrea, and Somaliland.

[f] Comprises Belgian Congo and Ruanda-Urundi.

[g] Comprises Angola and Mozambique (including territory of Manica and Sofala).

[h] Included in figures for specified countries.

DATA FROM CHAPTER VI COMPARED WITH OFFICIAL TRADE
FIGURES, 1937[a]—*Continued*

Country	Chapter VI		Officially Reported	
	Imports	Exports	Imports	Exports
Syria and Lebanon................	40	23	43	21
Turkey.........................	92	109	92	111
Arabia[i]...........................	22	18	27	15
Iraq...............................	41	88	48	28
Iran...............................	52	151	53	137
British controlled (not given above):				
India and Burma[j]................	560	983	577	825
British Malaya..................	372	512	405	520
Ceylon.........................	89	115	91	116
All other[k].......................	13	42	27	42
French controlled (not given above)[l]..	66	131	66	110
Netherlands East Indies.............	269	626	274	525
Japanese Empire[m]..................	1,137	990	1,139	956
Manchukuo and Kwantung[n].........	255	157	256	186
China and Hongkong[o]..............	398	392	402	285
Siam.............................	51	89	51	76
Philippine Islands..................	109	159	109	152
Total Asia......................	3,641	4,622	3,750	4,144
OCEANIA:				
Australia.........................	498	685	503	590
New Zealand......................	223	288	223	257
Other Oceania[p]....................	12	25	17	19
Total Oceania...................	733	998	743	866

[i] Imports in both columns and exports as officially reported are for Aden only, and in the main apparently represent transit trade destined for, or originating in the several states of the Arabian peninsula. Chapter VI export data include trade of other Arabian states—Hejaz, Nejd, Yeman, Oman, etc.

[j] Excluding trade between Burma and India; partly estimated.

[k] Comprises North Borneo, Brunei, Sarawak, Papua, Gilbert and Ellice Islands, Solomon Islands, New Guinea, and Nauru.

[l] French Indo-China, and French establishments in India.

[m] Includes Japan proper, Chosen (Korea), and Taiwan (Formosa). The three are treated as a unit, that is, the trade of each part with the other two parts is excluded.

[n] In the trade statistics for 1929 shown in Chapter VI the trade of Manchuria and Kwantung is included with China.

[o] China and Hong Kong are treated as a unit. The trade of the latter, although it is a British Crown Colony, is made up mostly of trans-shipments to and from the interior of China. (No Hong Kong statistics were available for 1929, but reasonably close estimates of imports by country of origin were made for Chapter VI based on export data of countries shipping to Hong Kong.)

[p] Comprises New Caledonia and other French settlements in Oceania, and the following British islands, Fiji, Tonga, Samoa, and New Hebrides.

Data from Chapter VI Compared with Official Trade
Figures, 1937[a]—*Continued*

Country	Chapter VI		Officially Reported	
	Imports	Exports	Imports	Exports
WESTERN HEMISPHERE:				
Canada and Newfoundland..........	832	1,146	833	1,016
United States.....................	3,081	3,408	3,083	3,349
Mexico...........................	174	145	175	176
British West Indies, and British Honduras[q]...........................	93	86	102	68
Other Central America[r]..............	72	70	76	64
Cuba.............................	129	187	130	186
Other West Indies[s].................	198	260	200	199
South America:				
Argentina......................	482	955	482	758
Bolivia.........................	21	34	22	44
Brazil..........................	330	384	334	348
British Guiana..................	10	15	12	13
Chile...........................	88	188	88	195
Colombia.......................	96	98	96	86
Dutch and French Guiana.........	5	6	6	5
Ecuador........................	11	19	12	15
Paraguay.......................	8	8	9	8
Peru...........................	59	112	59	92
Uruguay........................	45	72	45	55
Venezuela......................	86	192	86	236
Total South America............	1,241	2,083	1,251	1,855
Total Western Hemisphere.....	5,820	7,385	5,850	6,913
WORLD TOTAL.......................	26,962	26,962	27,310	25,092

[q] Comprises Bermuda, British Honduras, and 10 islands or groups of islands in the British West Indies for which trade data were reported in the *Statistical Abstract for the British Empire*, 1929 to 1938 (Trade and Commerce Section). Inter-island trade is excluded.

[r] Comprises Costa Rica, Guatemala, Honduras, Nicaragua, Panama, and El Salvador.

[s] Comprises Martinique, and Guadeloupe (French); the Territory of Curacao (Dutch West Indies), Dominican Republic, and Haiti.

EXPORTS OF MANUFACTURES

The manufactured goods exported from Nazi Europe include the products offered by the German chemical and machine industries and by Swiss watch and instrument makers, the perfumes and soap of France, and the fabrics, china, and glassware in which some of the coun-

PRINCIPAL CLASSES OF MANUFACTURED EXPORTS, 1937[a]
(Exports for 7 industrial countries, in millions of dollars)

Commodity Groups	Germany	Total for 7 Countries[b]
Chemicals, including fertilizers...............	188.5	329.6
Drugs, dyes, and paints.....................	139.9	214.4
Perfumes and soap..........................	12.5	34.4
Paper......................................	43.0	109.0
Fabrics of wool, silk, cotton, and artificial fibers..	99.7	422.1
Apparel....................................	52.3	138.9
Earthenware and china......................	27.3	43.2
Glass and glassware.........................	34.6	87.7
Iron tools, cutlery, and other iron manufactures..	215.9	300.0
Machinery, of all kinds.....................	426.9	586.3
Vehicles, including ships, automobiles, etc.......	147.9	257.9
Instruments and watches....................	74.4	142.3
Books and pictures[c]........................	14.1	20.8
Jewelry....................................	—	78.4
Yarns......................................	41.0	172.7
Total for manufactures listed...............	1,518.0	2,937.7
Total exports of manufactures..............	1,950.3	3,923.0
Exports of manufactures from the whole area..	—	(4,470.6)
Total exports of all kinds..................	2,376.4	5,679.5
All exports from the whole area..............	—	(8,422.0)

[a] Compiled from League of Nations, *International Trade Statistics*, 1938.
[b] These countries are: Germany, Austria, Belgium-Luxemburg, Czechoslovakia, France, Italy, and Switzerland.
[c] The total figure given for books and pictures is incomplete.

tries specialize. The general character of these exports is shown by the table on the preceding page.

The 15 broad classes of manufactured goods included in this table, taken together, accounted for 75 per cent of all exports from the 7 countries of Europe that normally are net exporters of manufactures and net importers of food and raw materials. Total exports of these commodities from the 7 countries concerned accounted for 65 per cent of the manufactured goods exported from the whole area, and for 35 per cent of Nazi Europe's total exports of all kinds.

INDEX

INDEX

Date Due